From

To A Hard Place

To Strive, To Seek, To Find, And Not To Yield

By

James Watts

Copyright © 2017

FROM ROCKY TO A HARD PLACE

One man's life of working in the front line as a Firefighter and Policeman.

Exeter and Bristol

1960's to 1990's

TO STRIVE, TO SEEK, TO FIND, AND NOT TO YIELD

(Ulysses Tennyson)

Our lives are full of everyday events but it's usually only the foolhardy, funny or frightening ones that are remembered. For some, these memories are so graphic that they are relived in dreams or nightmares, and for Jim, putting them down on paper has been helpful in some way and a step towards understanding the medical diagnosis of Post Traumatic Stress Disorder.

Relive with him, the fascinating tales of life as a Firefighter, Policeman and then Dog Handler in 'From Rocky to a Hard Place'.

Table of Contents

The Battle Field

Boxing Night Fight

"999 emergency which service do you require?"

"Police send the police to The Site. The gypsies are at it and there's going to be trouble."

Radios then buzzed into life " Any units able to drive by The Site, anonymous caller reporting some sort of disturbance."

I heard one patrol respond and knowing the location, I made my way to back them up with Rocky in the rear of the van. Rocky was one of the larger black and tan German Shepherds on the section weighing over one hundred pounds, and was a force to be reckoned with, despite his long haired coat and floppy ears giving him the appearance of a friendly teddy bear. The group were used to me turning up unannounced to support them as I always monitored the radio, and often the sight of the dog van was enough to calm a situation by swaying the balance in favour of the Police. Also, if I found that the dog was required to search or track, by turning up quickly I was able to take advantage of the freshest scent and get good results.

As usual, on this particular Boxing night I was one of the first units to attend and parked at the roadside gate of a hedged field. Visibility was virtually nil but the sound of many men's voices shouting abuse came from two sides of the field and there was potential for the situation to escalate. I called up another dog handler and my colleague arrived from a neighbouring division and, although a patrol car and some traffic cars attended, we were best placed and trained to assess the uncertain situation. With our dogs on leads we entered the field, our torches illuminating hot barking breath condensing as it hit the cold night air, and then shining on figures in the distance. The shouting quietened as they noticed our approach and I began to call out for them to calm down and go home. We had dogs and it made sense for them to listen and do as they were told, or they would be worse off. It's Christmas after all and the season of good will.

As the men gradually realised we were Police the shouting resumed, but now it was directed at us.

The group nearest us became more aggressive and in the faint light from dwellings beyond, the silhouettes of men wielding poles and sticks approached us with their bare chests reflected in our torchlight. Our dogs were barking at movement around us and it was soon apparent that the second group had circuited the field to become one unit of up to forty drunk aggressive men.

Initially four or five of them approached, wielding their weapons and they were warned.

"Put the stick down! Back off or we will use the dogs"

The dogs' training prepares them for stick attacks and they will protect their handler to the extreme.

As the men came closer Ray and I allowed our leads to lengthen and the dogs lunged out to disarm any attackers and then release their bite to take on the next one. The air was full of screams as teeth sank into arms legs and stomachs, with shouting and barking and the clang of scaffolding poles and sticks hitting home on both dogs and handlers. As each assailant fell to the ground a pair of figures emerged from the darkness to drag them away, and then others picked up the weapons to continue the assault. A broom handle snapped in two across Rocky's shoulders which did little to quell the adrenaline of a seriously switched-on dog. Each minute that passed seemed eternal as the unrelenting battle continued. Digger took the brunt of an iron bar smashing across his back and Ray took a head hit. He stood swaying from side to side and completely vulnerable, so I pulled up close to support Ray and grabbed Digger's lead whilst Rocky defended us all. Blue lights pulsated around and our radios called out reports of other units attending the affray, but they remained out of sight. To be fair, each with only a truncheon for protection and the likelihood of being bitten they were certainly in a safer place, but no help to us. I was vaguely aware of another call to our location reporting an ambulance being attacked. A man with a serious stomach wound had been placed in the first ambulance but someone decided to pull him out and continue their fight or maybe replace him with another injured assailant. About an hour after the chaos had begun the remaining men backed away.

By 4am I was at the station, attempting to make sense of what had happened, updating the Chief Superintendent who had been called in from his bed and who was horrified to hear the events and praised us for dealing with the gratuitous violence of the night. We were called to the front office where an older man was bitterly complaining about the injuries sustained by his family and others, and promising to put in an official complaint to the force. I assured him that anyone found to have been bitten would be arrested for attempted murder of a Police Officer, and he changed his tune.

A colleague told me that the Accident and Emergency Department at Frenchay resembled a scene from a battlefield with blood and bandages and bruised bodies. Forty one of those injured had dog bites, with five initially being detained in hospital and subsequently the police cells for the remainder of the holiday season until the Magistrates Courts resumed. Ray received treatment in the same hospital but fortunately in a different ward, and Digger also took some time to recuperate.

I met some of the boxing blokes about a year later, when two young officers attended a disturbance in a pub. I decided to give back up and found them looking in through the window at a drunk man who was being restrained by two other patrons. My arrival was a relief to the officers but exacerbated the situation when the drunk saw me and became even more aggressive. The two men bundled him out and into a vehicle and explained that the aggressive man had previously been bitten on the arm by Rocky and it had ruined a treasured tattoo.

If only he had "**P**ut **T**he **S**tick **D**own"

Where I come from

Growing Up

On reflection, I wonder why I put myself in so many challenging situations.

As a child my Saturday highlight was to visit the Premier Cinema in Bristol's Gloucester Road, and watch the latest cowboy films featuring John Wayne. I lived with my Grandparents in a terraced side street, and often paired up with my slightly younger cousin who lived nearby, and we would reenact the scenes we had watched. On one occasion I threw a noosed rope over the t-bar near the top of a street lampost, looped it over my cousin's head and pulled him up by the neck. Luckily we were stopped before any damage was caused and my John Wayne moments were put on hold, for quite a while.

Teenage years saw me growing up in Cornwall and South Devon working at a caravan camp site where I learned to drive and manoeuvre trailers, and then as a labourer for Costains who were installing drainage at Dawlish Warren. Irish navvies were paid by the yard for hand digging trenches in the sandy soil, which filled with water and were quite unstable, but my job was to light the safety lanterns and do odd jobs. I remember looking at the progress made by the two teams that had commenced from each end of the trench, and my rows of lighting didn't seem to line up. Sure enough, they were completely off set and had to be redug into even less stable earth. A good example of a failure to double check or 'measure twice and cut once'.

Dawlish Sands Holiday Park was home to Rebel, a large German Shepherd owned by the manager, and a dog that had freedom to roam within the site and guarded the place at night. He slept in the site Land Rover parked outside the caravan where I lived with my grandparents who were employed in maintenance and catering. In winter the camp was virtually empty so it was unusual to hear Rebel barking in the middle of the night, and when my torchlight picked out a figure pinned against the hedge, at sixteen and unsure how to handle the situation, I ran outside and called for the dog to stop. The man had his arms full and every time he tried to move, Rebel snapped closer, but when the dog turned back towards me the man dropped his haul of copper wire and ran through the hedge to escape.

Rebel was afraid of nothing on earth and I often took him with me when I went fishing from the rocks at night. On one walk home in the moonlight I decided to take a familiar route over a railway bridge at Dawlish Warren. As I reached the bottom step of the bridge Rebel stood still and refused to go any further, so getting nowhere with him I turned and took another path home. A while later I happened to be talking to a local resident who mentioned a tragedy some years before when a youth had jumped from the bridge in front of a train. I could not say whether the two incidents were connected but the bridge did sometimes feel eerie, even in the day.

On another occasion my twelve year old brother was visiting and although I couldn't drive on the road, I was keen to give him a tour of the site. I told him to jump into the front of the Land Rover and I went around to the driver's side, unaware of a sleeping dog in the back. We all know to 'let sleeping dogs lie' and Rebel was a prime example of this when he woke up suddenly, saw a stranger and reacted before I had a chance to stop him. John's ear was left hanging by the lobe and after some basic first aid he was bundled into the manager's car and rushed to hospital. The surgeon who stitched him up was greatly concerned about such a dangerous dog bite, but when he heard the circumstances and realised that we owned the dog, he agreed to not make a complaint to the Police. My first of many!

Employment in Teignmouth at a screenprint works occupied me for while. My job was mix smelly acrylic paint and print colour charts for cosmetics companies such as Helena Rubenstein and Lentheric, but I really wanted excitement. A friend joined the American Army to fight in Vietnam, and I was keen to join the Royal Marines but my grandparents refused to sign the papers and though disappointed, I soon learned that my friend had sadly become collateral damage in a foreign war zone. I still sought a challenging career and considered joining the local police force. My father had been a policeman and he talked me out of it but suggested trying the Fire Brigade, as they were allowed to sleep on quiet nights! and the public were always pleased to see a fireman.

Auxilliary Fire Service

At sixteen I was too young to be a regular fireman but in the interim I joined the Auxilliary Fire Service and paraded on sunday mornings, riding my NSU Quickly moped from Dawlish Warren to Exeter in uniform, prepared to join the duty watch for the day. A minimum requirement for full time fireman was to have a thirtysix inch chest with an expansion of two inches and I was scrawny but strong. I regularly got someone to measure my chest and then I'd breathe in as deeply as possible and measure again. That two inch difference was hard to achieve but I worked hard and trained when possible and enjoyed being part of a crew as an Auxilliary.

One memorable task was to move a convoy of twenty Green Goddess WW2 fire engines, from Exeter to a large Home Office storage facility in Temple Cloud, Somerset, a distance of about 40 miles. The old vehicles were due to be moth-balled as there was no likelihood of invasion and no need for the outdated Civil Defence Force in 1965 so the 4.9 litre petrol engines were on the move. Escorting the convoy were two motorcycles that rode up and down the line to check all was well and pass on information as there were no radios to communicate between the vehicles. The first vehicle to breakdown was marked with a yellow flag and left at the roadside, whilst the motorcyclist used a public phone to report the location for a recovery team to attend. The second vehicle had the same marker and then the third and the route became dotted with ten yellow flagged vehicles. Thankfully I was in one of only ten vehicles that reached the destination without breaking down. But it wasn't the last time that I would see a Green Goddess.

Firefighting Exeter

Fire Brigade Training

Eventually I met the requirement and was accepted to train as a full time fireman. Training was all about knowing the necessary information to tackle a task and to work with a team whose life depended on you and your's on them. I gained an understanding and respect for the value of Maths, English and Science that had escaped me during years of education when I skived off at any opportunity. This was learning for a purpose and I put every effort into achieving a result.

I was proud as punch at being appointed as a newly recruited fireman and was given the brigade collar number 48. Surrounded by the larger Devon County, Exeter was a small brigade and the city also had its own police force and ambulance service for a population of only about eighty-five thousand. How times have changed.

As a new recruit I was sent to the Surrey Fire Brigade Training School in Reigate on a fourteen week intensive course covering all aspects of fire fighting.

One exercise was a live carry down which involved running to the top of a fifty foot escape ladder and going in through a window to pick up another fireman, who was lying on the floor acting as an injured and unconscious person, then getting him onto your shoulders and carrying him down the ladder. It was very strenuous and dangerous stuff and the worst part of the drill was to act as the body and to be slung over someone's shoulder, looking straight to the ground. In the those days health and safety didn't exist and no safety harness was used. We were told that only weeks before my course, a fireman who was being carried down was killed because he grabbed the rounds (rungs) of the ladder and slid off the back of the carrier.

I passed the course and returned to start my new career in Exeter at eighteen years of age, was posted to "Blue" watch and eventually became a driver having passed courses in HGV driving, Breathing Apparatus, and operating a one hundred foot turntable ladder, now known as an arial ladder. Before long I was in the thick of it and loved every minute.

1966

My first posting was Exeter Fire Station covering the City and surrounding areas, situated in Danes Castle adjacent to the prison in the heart of Exeter.

I was now prepared to be one of those people who run into the burning building when everyone else is running out of it. Fired with enthusiasm, my first operational callout was a (non-fire) special service call raised by the RSPCA. Near the station in Bury Meadow Park a cat sat at the top of an oak tree and refused to come down. Tasked with the job of climbing the extension ladder, I rescued the cat and brought it safely to the ground handing it to the RSPCA officer. By that time the sight of a fire engine had attracted a large crowd including local press reporters. A lady emerged from the crowd offering her hand which I was about to shake when she said "Please accept this for rescuing my cat" and thrust a one pound note into my hand, as a camera shutter clicked, recording the moment.

I was aware of regulations prohibiting acceptance of payment of any kind from the public, and ensuring the photographer heard correctly, I loudly advised the grateful cat owner to donate the money to the Fire Brigade Widows and Orphans fund at the station.

A Baptism Of Fire January 9th 1967

After morning drill and equipment maintenance I was at the top of the sixty foot high drill tower checking radioactive material stored in a lead box and kept for training purposes. From my vantage point I had a clear view down toward the prison complex and noticed smoke billowing from within a building. Before I had the chance to alert anyone, the station alarm rang and I descended multiple ladders within the tower and raced to take my crew seat on the first of three appliances within the sixty second turn-out time.

The fire was in a storeroom of paint, rush mats, hemp, jute and canvas used by less extreme prisoners to sew into mailbags and other items. Wearing breathing apparatus we entered the storeroom and within fifteen minutes had the blaze under control. Mailbags and rush mats were stacked twenty feet high and thirty feet deep, and a pocket of fire was discovered about six foot into the stack. I was first in line of a chain comprising twenty men (firefighter to prisoner to prison officer), who commenced removing the smouldering materials. I reached up to a seven foot high pile of heavy jute mats and turned to pass an armful of them to the prisoner next in line. My last memory was his face looking up above me in horror as the highest piles of stock toppled and crashed down over me.

According to reports, I was buried with only the heel of one boot showing and when the first prisoner attempted to pull me out, my leather knee length boot came free empty.

Waking up in hospital I felt extremely grateful for the swift action of my colleagues, and those from the prison who had undoubtedly saved the first of my 'nine' lives.

April 1968

Training never stops and implementation of new regulations and revision of all aspects of firefighting are essential for an efficient service. One particular station officer was studying for the Institute of Fire Engineers qualification and whilst revising for that, he would test us all in hydraulic formulae. (The study of movement of water in motion and at rest.) Such as, a tank of water of a given dimension, or, a pond of unknown variable depth, would take how long to pump out using a particular capacity pump. The whole watch would assemble in a lecture room and half way through scribing a formula the Officer would turn and throw his chalk and whoever it hit was expected to complete the writing. A good way to learn and maintain attention.

Two years after becoming a fireman I was eligible to sit the leading fireman's examination which I passed on 10th April 1968 and then passed the practical test at a later date. Promotion, however, was reliant on a vacancy becoming available and a small station had only one leading fireman on each watch.

Other 'Nine Lives'

Attending a ground floor warehouse fire there was a possibility of someone being in the rooms above and I had climbed a ladder to the first floor carrying a hose reel and wearing breathing apparatus. It was difficult to see through thick smoke as I steadily skirted the edge of a room searching for any occupant. I had checked one wall and turned a corner, moving in darkness towards the middle when with little warning, the first floor ceiling completely collapsed. I plummetted down into the seat of the fire below with my temperature rising from fear and heat, as flames were beginning to engulf me. Two powerful hose jets of water were simultaneously directed into the fire and I was never more pleased to get a soaking. I managed to scramble out, grateful to my colleagues for their good timing and returned to the station for a change of kit and underwear, before going back on call, counting my blessings.

Another Warehouse

A long, narrow, single-storey warehouse containing cardboard and stationery, had smoke issuing from the door frame. After donning breathing apparatus, a colleague and I entered a smoke filled room and moved forward laying a knotted rope-line at waist height to mark our route. The rope has pairs of knots; a long knot denoting forward and a smaller knot indicating the way out. Making slow progress we almost reached the fire but due to low air supply, we left the line and followed the short knot out. Returning made for quicker progress as we could feel our way to safety, but that was until the rope fed downwards and we realised that a wall of cardboard had fallen, blocking our exit from floor to ceiling. We both set off our emergency distress alarms, assuming they could be heard from outside, but my air guage showed red with roughly five minutes of air remaining.

We urgently pulled at the obstruction as our reserves of air diminished and after a couple of minutes we detected movement and lights as our colleagues reached us twenty five yards from the entry door. With the last five yards remaining to reach the exit, my set ran out of air and the mask began to collapse onto my face. A lucky escape!

Flash Over

The Countess of Idesleigh had called the brigade to attend her large old Manor House near Exeter and on arrival we found a wing of the property well alight. Wearing breathing apparatus, our crew reached a long corridor at the top of a staircase. As we knelt with hose jets to receive instruction from the station officer, an escalation of the fire caused a flash-over which engulfed him in flames, melting his face mask, and also injuring others near me. I was unscathed on that occasion.

Hospital Fire

Fighting fire at Exeter City Hospital, it was discovered that the beds were too wide to push through doorways. A confused elderly patient had attempted to boil a kettle over an open fire which he had created on his bed. Mattress and curtains were alight and patients attached to intravenous drips had to be removed to safety. Adding to the pressure of this serious incident, each bed had to be tipped at enough angle to get it through the doorway, so patients were lifted out and then eventually resettled into their beds in another part of the hospital. Beds were queued up with patients in various states of ill health and distress, waiting to be removed from the smoke. Once the fire was out, there was plenty to do for all hands, damping down and clearing smouldering debris.

Tragic House Fire

On another occasion, near the hospital, a fire was noticed in a terraced dwelling by an off duty fireman. Beaten back by flames he was unable to rescue the occupants. Two small children had been asleep on a sofa in front of the fire, left there by their parents who had gone to the pub. The whole watch were affected by the anger and emotion surrounding this event and the sight of those children's remains melted into the furniture springs, stayed with us all.

Particularly Tragic Speeding Drivers

Early one summer's morning a large articulated lorry carrying telegraph poles had broken down on the rise out of a dip on the Exeter bound A38 near Wellington. At about 5a.m. a Triumph Herald car carrying a young family of four, failed to stop and travelled underneath the lorry at such a speed that it was completely flattened. We surmised that the driver had fallen asleep or was dazzled by the rising sun. Our emergency tender was dispatched with specialist equipment to help free those trapped and the damaged car was winched back out from beneath the very heavy cargo carrier. Despite our objective, it was obvious that no-one could have survived the impact, and the complete vehicle was removed to be dismantled with care at a police station. Our crew returned to Exeter in silent contemplation.

A38 Willand Straight was the location of another serious accident; A head on collision of a lorry and saloon car resulted in the deaths of a family of five who were thrown into, under and around the vehicles. Seat belts were not fitted or compulsory in those days. The roast lunch, that we had been about to tuck into prior to the call, remained uneaten that day.

A Funnier Side

When there was a chimney fire, older properties with multiple stacks required identification of the relevant chimney. Tall Victorian chimneys were too long for rods and stirrup pump so I had a hose reel on a roof where four chimneys emitted smoke. I dropped a pebble down inside and heard a shout which I took to be a positive response from a colleague so directed the hose into that chimney. After just thirty seconds I heard a lot of shouting from below so I turned off the water and climbed down to determine the problem and my amused colleagues told me to look inside at my handiwork. A family of six sat at a table set for their Sunday roast. Everything in the room; the walls, floor, ornaments, people, food, cutlery, the once white tablecloth and even the white Scottie dog, were all completely sooty black. A bit of a 'Delboy' moment. I should have checked twice!

Firefighting Gloucestershire

1971

Qualified and eager for promotion, I began applying for posts in other areas and transferred to the larger Gloucestershire Fire Service which held greater opportunity for me as a fireman. The vacancy was at a two pump, day-manning station in the new town of Yate with large housing estates and shopping precinct. Weekday eight-to-five shifts manned the first pump, retained part-timers manned the second pump and everyone covered the other times on-call, so the job came with a house nearby.

I had been out on a shout when a second call came in and was back at the station to see the retained crew return with their vehicle, but something wasn't right. The crew reported having dealt with their call, but they were shocked when I pointed out the empty sets of rollers on top of the fire engine where a thirty-five foot wooden extension ladder should have been secured. Retracing their route onto the dual-carraigeway they found the missing equipment, lying undamaged at a T junction where they had stopped momentarily, and were able to put it back onto the roof, remembering for always, the essential clamp.

One super-fit Station Officer put us through our paces and had us practising the carry down in reverse. We had to carry a 'body' up the ladder and down again, and then continue various obstacle circuits of the drill yard and station whilst wearing breathing apparatus that had to be removed and pushed in front in order to crawl beneath each fire engine. The final task was a simple knot tying exercise which always proved to be challenging when exhausted and starved of oxygen. On one particular day the Station Officer announced that after attending hospital for a vasectomy operation, he would return to take part in the training exercise as usual. With a measure of doubt we awaited his arrival and were highly amused when he rolled up in a wheelchair, fit for nothing.

Parked Tender Situation Distraction

Being close to the M4 motorway call-outs were often to road traffic accidents, and the residential area called us to chimney and chip pan fires. Being prepared for anything meant that everything was checked. A fire engine went out with full crew to check that street fire hydrants were unobstructed and in working order, and this aided our knowledge of topography too, but we were always available to attend any emergency call.

I was the driver on one cold February morning and, to leave plenty of room for traffic, had parked two thirds onto a verge near a brow at Westerleigh Road. I sat in the fire engine monitoring the radio for calls, and saw vehicles steadily approaching and slowing down from each direction. Whilst there was sufficient room for both to pass by, the drivers looked at the shiny red engine instead of concentrating on the road, and the two cars crashed head on beside me. Each appeared to contain a driver and adult passenger and one couple appeared to be uninjured. The driver of the other car got out and sat in the road dazed, but his female passenger ran across the field screaming and bleeding from a head wound from an impact which had shattered the windscreen. We all rushed to help and after reaching the woman as she collapsed, the senior officer sent me back for a first aid kit. As I passed the 'empty' car, I heard a baby whimpering. A carry cot wedged on it's side behind the front seats contained a six month baby whose blue face and hands matched his blue baby grow outfit. I carried the baby into the fire engine, wrapped him in my tunic, turned on the heating and commenced mouth to nose resuscitation and finger compressions, and used an aspirator to remove fluid, until an ambulance arrived with a doctor on board.

Prior to leaving to attend another emergency call, the exact position of our vehicle was marked on the road to aid Accident Investigators. Eventually traffic offence charges were not brought against me and I was thanked for the first aid I had given. One may assume that the shocked parents' first concern would have been for their baby in the back of the car, but though this baby was not a newborn, it was his first day of adoption. He survived in hospital for just a few months.

Firefighting Bristol

1974 Bristol

Ongoing training saw me pass the Sub Officer examination and practical test making me eligible for promotion to Leading Fireman. With a change of County boundaries, Yate in South Gloucestershire, became part of the new county of Avon along with Bristol City and North Somerset. Becoming a Leading Fireman at Temple Back Headquarters, in the centre of Bristol, gave me more challenging experiences and in fact, on my first night shift I was expecting the station's average eight callouts and we actually had a surprising sixteen shouts.

Temple Back, as the name suggests, was built on land historically linked to the Knights Templar. During the building of the fire station, after the removal of old burial remains, there had been a fatality of a construction worker and there were rumours of strange occurrences. On my shift a member of control room staff complained of someone playing a practical joke, wearing a white sheet and jumping out scaring her, but after rechecking every locked door and window everyone was accounted for and no intruders were found. A similar incident was reported a couple of weeks later and on another evening a fireman witnessed ghostly images fighting in the yard. A quiet member of the crew set about enquiring if the sightings were relevant, and a few of us sat around a table with our forefinger on a glass surrounded by the alphabet and numbers. In all seriousness, the glass moved while one person wrote down which letters were indicated. Amongst the notes it read TNTPARKSIRA...PARKS. Well, there are a lot of parks in Bristol!

At the time there was anti British terrorism and major cities had been targeted, and within weeks we were called to a possible gas explosion at the bottom of Park Street. We stopped our fire engine at a distance half way up the hill and whilst climbing out to assess the situation, a second explosion in an adjacent doorway, rocked the vehicle, injuring some of the crew and also injuring Police and Ambulance crews attending the call. It was confirmed that bombs had been planted by a known terrorist organisation. A lucky escape again, and when another 'message' told me to check my car and I half-heartedly kicked the wheels, a hub cap fell off along with three of the four wheelnuts !

Potentially Terrifying Ship Disaster

Avonmouth had its own fire station but major incidents required a predetermined attendance by Temple Back and I was in charge of a crew called to assist a ship fire in the docks. The cargo of peanuts and also the cabin area were both alight, creating large volumes of smoke which necessitated the use of breathing apparatus. Of seven appliances some included retained part-timers, and two crews had searched and reached two levels down into the ship, having left their 200ft guideline for my crew to follow. Thousands of gallons of water were being pumped into the vessel and a device (a transverse metacenter) on deck monitored the angle of list, and would alert if the ship was likely to turn turtle.

My crew continued seeking the seat of the fire, aware of an increasing amount of listing with every unsteady step along the dark, smoke-filled, narrow, 'tween-deck' passages, slopping with water. Nearing the end of our additional guide line and with low air supply, I was considering withdrawing to allow the next crew to take over, when we heard an air-horn which signalled 'abandon ship'. That was not what we wanted to hear being three decks down in smoke and darkness, but controlling our fear we quickly made our escape. On deck we found an unconcerned crew preparing to take our place, joking about the part-timer who had accidentally sounded the two tone horns on his fire engine!!

Despite our wished intentions, the culprit survived.

Police Bristol

A Change Of Career

As a Junior Officer I earned a place at Morton in the Marsh Officer Training College. I was doing well, but discord was brewing nationally across the service. Many staff and students took industrial action, and the establishment was closed, so I was instructed to return to Bristol. My Chief Fire Officer was not impressed as that order had not come from him.

Rostered annual leave was always welcome and on return from one holiday I was surprised to hear from a neighbour, that a Senior Fire Officer had called to my home address.

I contacted the station to be told that the boss had indeed called to offer me the promotion I'd been waiting for, but as I was not at home, the rank of Sub Officer had been given to someone else. Really??

Feeling dissillusioned with the fire service, and working in Bristol alongside Avon and Somerset Constabulary, I renewed my original thoughts of becoming a policeman. With family responsibilities, not everyone around me thought it was a good idea, but in December 1975 I joined the police and, after training, was posted to D division Lockleaze, as a rookie. Not an easy task after being used to a supervisory role and, after eighteen months, I questioned my decision and attempted to return to the fire service. Though I was offered a place in Gloucestershire, I then decided to not quit before completing my two year police probation, and would see if the job improved, which it did.

New Beginning

Lockleaze was a lively station, with the D division radio control room, cells, front office and CID department commanded by a Chief Inspector. I easily passed authorisation to drive a Panda car and also the Rocks Rescue vehicle, and later a motorcycle course.

The 1970's saw Britain face industrial action by many national organisations, including the fire service. The old 'Green Goddess' engines were recommissioned to provide emergency cover and some were based at the Territorial Army base, on my patch in Horfield. A single crewed police unit was sent each day to direct military fire crews who were unfamiliar with the area and civilian type incidents. Of course, I could not stand back and just watch potential errors being made, and so supervised and instructed the fire teams accordingly. Ex-colleagues picketing at the TA centre, complained that I was over-stepping my authority as a Policeman, and undermining their industrial action. To my frustration, though sworn to protect life and property as a Constable, I was soon reassigned duties. Such was the power of the unions. (However, I may have given passing attention to any fire incident on my patch).

I missed some of the cameraderie of a close knit team in the fire brigade, and it seem strange to be single crewed and solely responsible for my allocation of calls. Of course there were colleagues and supervisors on the shift who could be called for back up or advice when necessary.

The Bunko Squad

The group had changed personnel and after listening to me talking about my wooden clinker-built 12 foot dinghy, a few younger new recruits agreed to a fishing trip. A week of nights had finished and one way to readjust to normal sleep pattern was so stay awake on the first morning. So at 6a.m. we jumped into my car, and with the boat trailer hooked onto the tow bar, headed to Lyme Regis. I had taken the precaution of checking the weather conditions with the harbour master who had said force 4-5 was expected but staying near to shore shouldn't be too bad. We put to sea and the outboard motor chugged us into the bay. As long as I focused on the horizon I was fine, but my colleagues were setting mackerel lines and hooks and bailing out the water. There were complaints of "I thought you said you'd waterproofed this old boat" and " I feel sick"

I told them that a dry boat needed to get wet to expand and fill the gaps, but the water level remained despite frantic use of the old baked bean tin. The sea became very choppy and with half my crew suffering 'mal-de-mer' and with a catch of one single small fish, we decided to about-turn. That was when the outboard motor conked out. I leaned out, removed the spark-plug to dry it and when returning it almost dropping the plugspanner into the deep. Once replaced the engine sparked into life but we had drifted in the increasing off-shore wind which matched the drive of the motor, so we were making no progress. By then we were all feeling ill and using the oars and the outboard, made a very slow return to shore. After lifting out one of our 'green' crew and laying him on the edge of the Cobb we set about pulling Bunko out of the water with an audience of local bearded fishermen standing with arms crossed. How embarrassing!

One chap said " What 've ye caught then?"

Keeping our single fish hidden I vaguely replied "Mackerel"

But then another chap looked interested and taunted me with "Oh? 'ow many?"

Not wanting to pursue the humiliation I kept my head down and said "Just one"

The fisherman smiled and, with an almost respectful nod said

"Well that's the only one caught off 'ere today"

With that, I proudly stretched out my hand and presented the day's haul, to a loud round of applause from the salty sea-dogs.

My crew slept through the return drive to Bristol and declined to arrange another trip.

Exhaustive Enquiries

Key to good policing was local knowledge of the area and it's inhabitants and using that to my advantage.

Theft of an exhaust pipe was one of my crime reports and the complainant told me that it had a unique identity mark. On patrol I noticed a ropey old vehicle with a newly fitted exhaust so crawled underneath the car with a torch and found the mark as described. The vehicle belonged to a young man known to the station so I knocked on his front door and told his mother that I needed to speak to her son about a noisy exhaust.

She told me he was out but he'd recently had the exhaust fixed and it wasn't noisy now. So that she didn't have the neighbours seeing police coming to her house again, I suggested that she send her son up to the local station to speak to me. When he confidently arrived and told me where he'd bought the part, I told him what I knew and he admitted the crime.

Getting A Cough

On another occasion I happened to call into the station where a DC had been unsuccessfully interviewing a female suspect for a while. She was a 'regular' and as she knew me, I asked if her troublesome boys (by name) had laughed about what she'd done. 'Yes' she said 'They pissed 'emselves laffin' when I walked in with the gear.' A lovely admission of guilt.

Fair Cop

A particularly aggressive drunk had refused to pay his taxi fare and had gone into his local pub where most of the patrons knew me and I knew them. When I arrived, the man was intent on fighting, but the locals held him back and offered to pay the fare if I agreed to not arrest him. The taxi driver was happy to not press charges as long as he was paid, so they had a whip round of everyone in the pub, including the landlord, and the matter was settled.

TV Producer

A quiet single crewed night patrol could get boring with not much happening and no-one to talk to. One such night I spotted a local villain carrying a small television set along the pavement not far from the police station. He saw me and immediately stopped. I recognised him straight away as I had dealt with him for years for various offences and we were on first name terms. He was a likeable rogue and I knew where to find him if I needed to speak to him about local crime issues. He said that he had removed the TV from a skip which was in the road not far away. I knew this was true because I had noticed it earlier on my patrol but I thought I would have a bit of fun and I asked him if he had a television licence for it. He looked blank. There was a form that could be given to motorists requiring them to produce their driving documents at a police station, so I gave him form HORT1 to produce his TV licence at Lockleaze Police Station. He duly did the next morning much to the amusement of the officer on duty in the front office.

May The Force Be With You

This job had the potential to have turned out as multiple murder enquiry when a 999 caller reported that a man had strangled an elderly lady on the first floor of his block of flats. My crew mate and I were confronted by a four-storey block of flats, and as shouts and screams were coming from upper floors we ran in and straight up the stairs. On the first floor landing an unconscious woman lay by an open front door, but hearing screaming from the upper floor, we ran on up the stairs to find another unconscious woman lying by another open apartment door, and then further screams from above sent us flying up the stairs to find a long haired hippy-type male trying to strangle an elderly lady who was on the floor on her back and he had his hands firmly around her throat.

We dragged him off and applied handcuffs as other officers together with an ambulance arrived to assist with the mayhem. He fought all the way down the stairs and was so violent that my colleague sat on him on our short journey to the station. When we marched him in, he suddenly calmed down asking why we had arrested him and why had we taken him there. In the charge office we informed the station sergeant of the circumstances of the arrest, and as he had calmed down and there were three of us present, we removed the hand cuffs. In a split second he leapt up on the charge office table put both arms in the air and shouted "May the force be with you!"

The sergeant wasn't impressed so handcuffs went back on and he was straight into cells until we could work out what the hell was going on here.

A Police Doctor later examined him and learned that the prisoner had taken opium five years previously whilst in India and had not touched any since, but stated that with this type of drug a flashback can occur many years later. Criminal records were checked and he had no prior conviction for any crime recorded, and was generally of good character. When he eventually came back to normal, I nicer person you wouldn't find. I can't remember the outcome of the subsequent court hearing but I know that all the people who were assaulted by him, lived to tell the tale.

Papers To Signal Deportation

On my patch around the Ashley Down area of Bristol there were many rental properties let to mostly law-abiding, foreign students whose wealthy parents chose to invest in a British education. In fact Bristol is a multi-cultural city, and though primarily white British, has a wide diversity of population.

One summer evening a call came in that two men of Middle-Eastern appearance had threatened a passer-by with a large kitchen knife having a white handle that looked like animal bone.

I was dispatched to the scene and the informant had left prior to my arrival, but the two suspects were standing on the pavement outside their flat. I told them about the complaint and they denied any involvement and also denied owning a knife of the description given.

I searched them and found nothing but asked if they objected to me looking in their flat, and reluctantly they agreed. When I found a similar kitchen knife, they admitted frightening the informant who had been shouting abuse at them from the street below. I took possession of the knife and told them I would make further inquiries and any further proceedings would be by way of summons. I didn't want to nick them before finding out what the informant was up to and he was possibly not without blame too.

On my return to the station I submitted my report and was instructed to report the incident to HQ Special Branch who told me to fill out a deportation form and send it asap. I hadn't known there was such a form but I complied and when I returned to work after a couple of rest days, an order had been issued for their deportation and they were sent home within seven days.

Hell that's a bit rapid I thought, but I can't imagine that happening so quickly these days.

Indian Takeaway Table For One

Delta 2 covered the Gloucester Road with it's many pubs, restaurants and late night takeaways, and every night without fail there would be several calls regarding drunken behaviour either inside or adjacent to these premises. Some diners refused to pay for their meal which they had consumed and then said wasn't up to standard, but if they hadn't complained during the meal, as soon as the police arrived it would be settled straight away. Other calls were usually disorderly behaviour or damage to property due to drunken revelry.

One night a more unusual call sent me to an incident at an Indian restaurant/takeaway and though the details were sketchy my double crew colleague and I made our way there with every expectation of a typical job. However we arrived to the sound of blood curdling screams from within the restaurant and a male voice shouting,"Please! Please help, get an ambulance, I'm dying" The scene inside resembled a film set with restaurant staff armed with knives and a baseball bat, being loudly threatened by a group of middle aged men complaining about the plight of their friend. He was the source of all the screaming and the man sat at a blood soaked wooden table with a nine inch carving knife thrust through his left hand piercing it to the table and oozing blood everywhere.

I called for back up, told the staff to put down their weapons and the men to sit down and be quiet, and they all complied but the bleeding man was our priority. An ambulance crew quickly arrived and agreed that to pull the knife out would cause more damage and he could most likely bleed to death. So after a shot of morphine the patient was carefully moved, complete with table which we helped to carry and with the knife jarring no more than was absolutely unavoidable. Negotiating the ambulance doors was a challenge but without delay the task was completed and the vehicle sped away to hospital leaving us to make sense of what had happened.

The proprietor explained that in recent weeks a number of customers had left without paying and the injured diner was yet another who thought he could get away with it by being abusive, but the waiter was very annoyed and determined to stop him leaving. Not the best policy for customer relations, and as a result the restaurant was closed, the waiter was charged with wounding, and I believe the injured man recovered but probably thought twice about his behaviour in future.

Police Tackle Stops Dancing

Bristol Rovers' football ground at Eastville was also a venue for Speedway and Greyhound tracks and also housed an entertainment space. The same local people supported all the events but their rowdiness at football matches contrasted with their behaviour at cycle or dog races. What is it about football that brings so much aggressive behaviour?

The Doghouse Disco night club also created an amount of Police work, and having got to know the bouncers it became one of my regular tea stops. In a quiet spell on night shift at about one o clock I called by to give passing attention before the club kicked out, but a bouncer approached me in concern. "Jim we've got a problem, there's a bloke on the dance floor and he's got a gun in his back pocket."

In the spirit of John Wayne, I took off my hat, tunic and tie and stepped into the disco which was full of people displaying their 'John Travolta' dance moves to a track that may have been 'Staying Alive' by the Bee Gees. Sure enough amongst all the dancers was a man with a mexican moustache gyrating in an attempt to impress the females with his moves. As he turned, I caught sight of the black butt of a gun which by it's shape, looked like an automatic pistol. Not known for my dancing prowess, I sidled up and as the man turned away I grabbed him in a bear hug then walked him to the edge of the dance floor, where bouncers helped me to handcuff and search him, and remove the weapon.

By then the bouncer's 999 call had brought the troops in and having found car keys in the man's pocket, we searched for a corresponding vehicle and located a saloon car. In it's boot we found a number of cloth bank bags which held cash and some that were empty and, a check on the Police National Computer flagged up that the car had been seen leaving the scene of an armed robbery in Thames Valley. Result!

Taking The P.

My duty Inspector decided to accompany me on patrol and I commenced my night shift in Delta 3 which covered most of the Fishponds area of North Bristol.

The night was unusually quiet as we drove down the main Fishponds Road, until a call came in from a very unhappy resident about a noisy party in this very same road, but asked for us to not approach his house for fear of reprisal. The Inspector and I made our way slowly down the road and we could hear the noise from this party some distance away. I checked my watch and it was 1.30 am when we pulled up outside a large Victorian terraced house which appeared to be full of people shouting loudly and with very loud music, so we could understand the complaint.

Most times under these circumstances a quiet word with the occupier is sufficient to sort the problem out, but not tonight. The Inspector knocked on the door very loudly to no avail, but several people started looking out of the ground floor window and began giving us the V sign whilst shouting abuse.

A sash window suddenly opened and a youth urinated over the Inspector's uniform sleeve and then closed the window and moved away quickly into the large group within the room. Eventually after several minutes of door knocking the person running the party answered the door, and when we explained to him why we were there and also that someone had urinated over the Inspector, he and his fellow partyguests seemed to find it highly amusing.

When told that the person responsible was going to be arrested for damaging police property they tried to close the door but I intervened and blocked it open allowing the Inspector to continue.

"If he doesn't give himself up we are going to arrest everyone in the house until the matter is resolved."

I thought 'Hell boss how can we do that, there's about fifty people in there'

True to his word, every available police officer arrived at the house and the suspects were all frog marched under arrest into waiting police vans, but because of the numbers involved, they were distributed amongst every Bristol station which were numerous in those days. They were lodged until the guilty person owned up to his dastardly crime, creating a lot of paperwork and a lot of very unhappy station Sergeants having to get involved in a job that wasn't theirs. An admission of guilt didn't take long and his very unhappy friends were released without charge. At least the neighbours were eventually able to get some peace and quiet and a number of people learnt the meaning of zero tolerance.

Police Motorcyclist

Motorbike Crash Course

I have always had a great love of motorbikes and when the opportunity arose to become a police motorcyclist, I jumped at it. A two week course with a Police Traffic Motorcyclist tutor culminated in a written exam and a practical test which was a ride followed and observed by an examiner from a different division.

There were five of us on the course and on the Monday morning of the first week we were given our bikes. I thought this was great: June sun shine and getting paid to ride a motorcycle through the countryside of Avon and Somerset and occasionally drift into Devon. We all set off from Bristol like five ducklings being followed by Mother Duck.

We swapped around so a different rider could take the lead and it was always challenging if you were last in the line to catch up, especially if the traffic was heavy. On one occasion we were travelling along by Bristol airport in an area known as Brockley Combe which was quite wooded. As we rounded a bend one of our group left the road and disappeared at speed into the trees, and seeing this we all believed that he would have been quite badly injured. As we stopped at the main road junction he suddenly came flying out of the woods covered in branches, with a big grin on his face and to our surprise and relief, was completely unhurt.

The two sunny weeks were swift and enjoyable with no need for wet weather gear. On the last Thursday we all took our written test and passed with flying colours and the next day we had our final ride and were to be tested individually. I rode out, closely followed by a Police Examiner, riding to the system which I had been taught during the course, and was relieved when he congratulated me on a successful ride. We all passed and decided to take the scenic route back to Bristol through Nempnett Thrubwell down Awkward Hill. (Lyrics of The Worzels song 'Down In Nempnett Thrubwell' includes the line 'You never see a traffic cop' but I'm not sure if it was written before or after this particular day.) Riding down a very narrow country lane one behind the other, I was towards the back with the instructor behind me, when suddenly out of nowhere came an old saloon car travelling at great speed towards us. In an attempt to prevent injury, the bikes were dropped onto the road or hedge with engines revving at high speed. The instructor and I were lucky to have hung back a bit and remained upright. I couldn't believe what had just happened and we spent some time straightening gear change levers and tying up windscreens, headlights, fairings and bits of the bikes with baler twine, before limping home. This police accident was referred to as a *POLAC*, and on some occasions you were not allowed to drive until properly investigated by a supervisory officer. Within an hour of fully qualifying as police motorcyclists, four out of five were grounded. The driver of the car was a local farmer and always drove up the lane at that time and that speed, 'because no-one else was ever on the road', but it was deemed not in the public interest to prosecute him.

Pulling The Stupid Driver

Call sign Delta 8. On my first day out as a Police Motorcyclist it seemed strange not to be driving a car, but all round vision was better for spotting villains, negotiating traffic was easier and I quite enjoyed it, to begin with. As winter approached I often became very wet and cold, and questioned my decision to be on two wheels. Sometimes, especially dealing with road accidents, my hands were so cold I could barely hold a pen, and to keep a reasonable body temperature I wore thermal vest and long johns which were effective but unbearable if called into the centrally heated station office.

A police officer on a marked police bike is quite visible - you would think, but apparently not for one lorry driver in Station Road, Yate. I was riding at about thirty miles per hour when from a large factory to my left, an articulated lorry pulled out in front of me and there was no way I could stop in time. During the training course we had talked about this sort of scenario and had learned to drop the bike and try sliding away which I attempted to do. The bike slid under the artic and I bounced along with my back coming to rest against the rear wheel. The huge vehicle stopped momentarily and I made eye contact with the driver looking out of his window directly at me, but unbelievably he started to drive off. Fortunately uninjured, I jumped up, ran to the drivers cab door, found the engine isolater switch which was by his leg and stopped his escape. I pulled him from the cab and, after a short struggle, arrested him and he was taken to the station. After a conversation with his boss back in Yorkshire he was sacked and had to get the train back home. I was a qualified heavy goods vehicle driver, so drove the vehicle to a place of safety until it's collection, and the driver was charged with a string of motoring offences including assault on police.

A Fit Of Pique

The police bike had a radio fitted on the rear carrier with a wire connected via the handlebars to the motorcycle helmet allowing messages to be sent and received on the move. The white helmet was fitted a with press stud detachable peak which helped to deflect rain or shade bright sunlight so was never removed. One winter's evening I received a call to a disturbance at a Chinese restaurant on the Gloucester Road which was on my patch and I knew the proprieters, but I'd never had a problem with them before. In the doorway a youth stood shouting racist remarks and using foul language directed at the Chinese occupants. The shop owners were still holding the meat cleavers and large knives that they had been using to prepare food prior to the outburst from the youth and when I asked them, they immediately put the items down. However, the dim-witted youth was not prepared to give up so easily, and resumed his shouting and swearing whilst running towards me. The head butt I received came as a complete surprise to me and probably to him as well when he fell into an unconscious heap at my feet and my helmet peak flew through the air into the road. Unbelievable, but fortunately I had plenty of witnesses. A splash of water revived the youth and a police car arrived to take him to the station where I headed after refitting my helmet peak and appreciating the protection it afforded.

Passing Traffic Sheep Dip

At that time I also rode my own motor bike to work on D division, wearing police motorcycling gear. Still living in Yate, my route through Winterbourne was on a semi-rural undulating road, often subject to patches of autumn mist at lower levels. At 5.30a.m. one morning I approached a dip and through the mist, my headlight picked up hundreds of pairs of eyes from a flock of sheep blocking the road. The collision somersaulted me into the air, landing back to back on an animal, dislodging my helmet, and the bike ended up in a hedge with the motor revving until it cut out. I dragged myself to the verge and lying on my side, held up my white helmet to attract a passing motorist. The first car didn't stop but later on a campervan did, and I was helped into the back and taken to Frenchay hospital by the driver who had seen the sheep dispersing. A hairline skull fracture kept me in for observation for a couple of days, followed by some woolly-headed time off work. A couple of police officers from E Division interviewed me about the accident and they denied ever seeing sheep near that road, suggesting my riding skills were lacking, and they were less than helpful in getting my bike moved. On release from hospital I stopped at Winterbourne and found a field with sheep droppings and wool fragments and it's gate loosely held with baler twine. I contacted E Division and asked that they advise the farmer on their patch, that he was lucky to not be prosecuted. Surprisingly, when I eventually returned to duties and opened my locker, my spare uniform hung neatly beside a very large meat cleaver!!

I lived to tell another tale!

September 1977 Petrol Tragedy Several Dead

"There's been a nasty fire on your patch this morning Jim, with several fatalities"

Late turn had begun. The premises in Eastville was an Indian restaurant and one of my tea stops owned by an entrepreneur with whom I'd shared many friendly chats so I was saddened to think he had lost his life, and made my way to his shop to find out what was happening. The scene was one of devastation with a gutted, roofless building and damage to neighbouring businesses. I headed to the mobile incident office nearby and was happily surprised to see my aquaintance sittting drinking tea. He didn't live on the premises but had rented upper floor rooms to students who had all perished and he was distressed and in a state of shock.

My old firefighting colleagues were out in force and I checked through the building to see the indescribable consequences of the blaze which they believed had begun on the ground floor. There was a gas boiler with a timer, at the rear of the commercial kitchen, which was presumed to have been the cause of an explosion, and highly flammable linoleum floor tiles would have created additional caustic fumes and flames that reached the occupants before having a chance to wake up.

However, a questionable smell of petrol near the front door suggested foul play.

The owner was further visibly shaken and could think of no-one who would have done such a thing, so a multiple murder enquiry ensued, with Detectives investigating all those connected to the premises. They soon uncovered some relevant information about the proprieter, who had previously been charged with a minor arson offence after setting a small fire in his own premises with a view to claim an insurance payout.

The man was brought into the station and I was there as a friendly face to put him at ease, but sweat poured off him and he denied any involvement, 'as he had been asleep at home'. He professed to swear on his life that he was innocent and we were getting nowhere. In a final attempt of persuasion, we found a copy of the Quoran in the Chief Inspector's office, placed it on the table in front of our suspect, and asked him to swear that he was not responsible. He shook his head and said he could not, and when asked why he said " because I caused the fire".

He thought it would be a simple insurance job if a small fire started because someone would call the Fire Brigade and no one would be harmed. He hadn't anticipated a speedy escalation of the blaze from the various flammable products in the restaurant, and was charged with multiple manslaughter.

Prosecution Took Some Detection

As Delta 3 area Panda driver, one of the areas I covered from Lockleaze Police station was Vassals Park. I was sent to investigate when a Swan had been shot and killed in the park and its mate had been wounded, believed to be by an air weapon. The injured swan had been removed by the RSPCA and taken to Slimbridge bird sanctuary for treatment, but because Swans mate for life they said that it was unlikely to recover, and within a week it died.

This incident created a massive press release with headlines of 'Swan Killer at Large', and coverage continued for several days. Sir Peter Scott at Slimbridge had communicated with the Chief Constable and hoped the offender would be quickly brought to book, so I was ordered off my regular duties to concentrate on finding and arresting the perpetrator.

Where do I start, I thought and went straight to the scene of the shooting, looking for anyone who had witnessed this horrendous crime. Some teenagers in the woods told me they had seen a man about twenty five years old with an air-rifle, but had not seen him fire it, and knew roughly where he lived in a road not far from the woods. Checks via the Police National Computer on likely persons living in this street, found one man of similar age who had a conviction for armed robbery of a petrol station. At the address the door was answered by a middle-aged woman and when I explained why I was there she appeared very nervous, especially when I noticed a rifle, propped up against the wall in the hallway. She claimed it was not her son's but belonged to his friend and that her son was due back soon and to take it up with him. He didn't turn up so I removed the weapon as I believed it had been used to shoot the swans and on opening the rifle I found it loaded with a .22 pellet, so took it to the station to discuss with my sergeant what offences had been committed. Technically the Crown owns all unmarked Mute swans in open water, and the Queen only exercises her ownership rights on some stretches of the Thames and its tributaries. Other varieties of swan (Bewicks, Whooper,) aren't included in this. The swan in question was actually a Bewick. My enquiries revealed that the suspect had been sentenced to four years for robbery and was therefore prohibited for life from possessing any type of firearm and that includes an airweapon.

Other offences included, 'discharging a firearm in a public place' and the Wildlife and Countryside Act in relation to 'killing and injuring a bird'. The swans were fed and protected by Bristol City Parks Department and therefore were deemed to be their property, and in law, property can be damaged. My decision to apply the offence of 'criminal damage' to both swans, was initially questioned by senior officers, but when I produced a witness statement from the council confirming my thoughts on their ownership they agreed that that offence would also be appropriate. I later arrested the man who was charged with all the offences, remanded in custody, and later received three years imprisonment. The Judge commended me on my actions, I received a lovely letter from Sir Peter Scott, and the press were happy with "Swan Killer Jailed".

CID

CID Aide

I think it must have helped my cause to progress, as I soon commenced a three month attachment to CID. Initially I was given a pile of cases that the others had offloaded from their in-trays. Like a rookie again but I enjoyed the demanding level of working thoroughly to get a job done.

Brief Encounter

A prolific burglar had been detained again and had asked for his solicitor to attend at the station. A large quantity of stolen goods from the burglary had not been recovered but the burglar admitted his crime and asked whether the courts would look favourably on him if he returned the goods. Asked how that could happen he said his solicitor could organise it. The solicitor arrived and after speaking with his client he approached me and said that if all the stolen property mentioned was to appear along the wall at the front of the police station, would it help his client's case. I asked him how that was going to happen and he said he knew where the property was and he would bring it to the station.

I told him that "If you do that you will be arrested for handling stolen goods and also conspiracy to pervert the course of justice."

"Ahh we'll forget that then..... Ok. If you allow me to bring a takeaway curry for my client he will agree to have other offences 'taken-into-consideration'." (So he did, and we got the property back.)

In other words, he would admit to other outstanding crimes so as not be nicked for them later and it would tick off some of our list of reported offences. The theory was that a defendant pleading guilty and admitting a backlog of crimes would give an impression to the court that they had 'come clean' and were reformed characters, and it sometimes worked....until the next time.

Cell Division

At Lockleaze CID a detained prisoner had been processed and the paperwork completed before being taken to the Magistrates Court cells to be remanded in custody. I had searched the prisoner and found nothing on him, so I was surprised when an officer rang from the court to demand our attendance because our man had been found to have a knife. My mentoring CID colleague didn't have to tell me how serious the situation was and that my attachment to the department could be at an end, but he questioned whether my search had been thorough enough and I couldn't understand how I missed a weapon.

At the court, the cell officer was adamant that we were at fault, until they discovered that another prisoner who had been in the same cell was the source of the weapon and the failure to find it was down to someone else. That was relief.

I enjoyed working in CID so much, that when offered a permanent promotion to Detective I didn't hesitate in accepting. Unfortunately, the long irregular hours had impacted at home and family considerations meant that I returned to the shift as a uniform PC with some dissatisfaction, which later contributed to a change of family circumstances.

Incident Car

There In Black And White

I was an effective policeman using my local knowledge of the area and it's criminals, and became one of the new advanced driver Incident Car crew.

Leaving Lockleaze to collect some court papers from central Bristol, I was (jokingly) asked by a DC to issue a Summons as I was passing the address in the city. In uniform, I parked my shiny new police car outside the cafe address and, like John Wayne entering a saloon, saw every customer lift their newspaper or look down at their drink, with no-one making eye contact. The proprietor looked surprised as I demanded a signature for his son's summons to court, but not as surprised as the CID department when they heard that the summons had been served. The cafe and its occupants were infamous for trouble and aggravation and police rarely attended alone, especially in uniform.

Put Through Serious Discomfort

All was not well at a large public house in the St George area of North Bristol. This particular pub was well known for trouble and was regularly attended by the local police for anti-social behaviour and drunkenness. It was just after midnight on New Year's Eve and calls were coming in of a large fight which had spilled out into the street and side car park. It involved over sixty people, mainly men, but there were some women caught up in it as well. Many police were sent to the scene from all parts of Bristol and arrests were being made. I was solo crewed and quickly found myself surrounded. One 'Hells Angel type' threw a punch at me, which missed, but he then hit my chest with a drop kick, pushing me into a concrete wall which collapsed into a heap of rubble. Miraculously I scrambled up and grabbed his long hair, put him in an arm lock and dragged him to my police car where he was handcuffed and placed face down on the floor behind the drivers seat. I slid the seat back to prevent him from getting up or moving whilst I drove to the police station about a mile away, The last thing I needed was for him to break free and attack me whilst driving. I began to move off and had travelled about a hundred yards when I heard a banging noise coming from on top of my car and then suddenly an upside down face appeared at the driver's window. It was my prisoner's mate who was intent in stopping me travelling to the station. He must have been holding on to the blue light as there was nothing else on the roof. What an idiot! I 'slowed the vehicle down' and he tumbled off the roof and landed in a heap in the road behind me! Resuming my journey to the station I booked in my prisoner with the Sergeant who told me that a report had come in of a man lying in the road, and could I investigate on my way back to the pub as the fighting was continuing. Before I had a chance to explain, I passed out and collapsed to the floor, and woke up in the Intensive Care Unit of Frenchay Hospital (again). The kick had resulted in a badly bruised heart. Not a pleasant experience, but I seemed to make a full recovery and soon returned to duty.

Barking Mad

Schools were often targeted by disgruntled ex-pupils, so when the alarm sounded at Monks Park Comprehensive, I wasn't surprised to see two young adults climbing out of a window and running away at speed. My colleague and I gave chase on foot and though I shouted for them to stop they were getting away, much to my annoyance. A dog barking in a garden inspired me to mimic a dog bark and then shout that I was about to let the dog loose. My colleague looked over his shoulder thinking my 'bark' was real, and the two young men were also convinced and gave themselves up.

The dog section were unimpressed, thinking it undermined them, and would people believe they actually had a dog when warned in future.

The story made it into the police Newsbeat publication and was picked up by the press like the Sun and Star whose reporters contacted me for an interview, which I declined. My photograph featured in the morning papers with untrue quotes about being nicknamed Rover, and also reached Reuters News Agency reporting 'Unarmed cop arrests fleeing felons by mimicking dog bark'.

An initially suspect package, addressed to Officer Watts, Bristol City Police Department, turned out to be a can of maple syrup from a Canadian Funeral Director, who had read the story and asked if I could send a police badge to his collector friend in Tavistock Police, Ontario.

We later exchanged many letters and flew to meet him on an inaugural flight from Bristol to Toronto. With great hospitality the Krugs put us up for a few nights and we slept above the 'box room' full of huge elaborate satin-lined coffins. One morning our enthusiastic host showed us his work room with bottles and syringes and explained how to embalm a body, prior to his wife calling us for lunch.

They also arranged for us to meet personnel from Tavistock, Ontario Provincial, and Royal Canadian Mounted Police, at Punky Doodles Corner restaurant and, whilst a Canadian policeman of British heritage announced the ceremony by playing 'Scotland The Brave' on bagpipes, we exchanged police memorabilia.

Later that evening we all gathered for a question and answer session in their large 'visitation' room, normally used for paying respects to the departed. In the wake of Hillsborough, the Canadian Police were confused by our need to have a police presence at football matches. Was it not our national game supported by families? And why were there no seats for the crowds of supporters herded into separate 'cages' to watch a sporting match? Why indeed!

Dog Section Jason

Persevered To Specialist Department

A while later, having remarried and living in a Police house, I decided that I wanted to join the dog section. Bower Ashton was the HQ of the Mounted and Dog Section, where as a volunteer criminal where you were expected to run for the dogs and generally help with all aspects of training. After several sessions I believed this was the job for me.

I was eventually successful in my application in 1983, (the year seat belts became compulsory.) The basic course lasted thirteen weeks and covered disciplines such as tracking, search for person, gun attack, stick attack, crowd control, obedience and many other things.

The gifted dog allocated to me to train was called Jason AKA 'Exocet' (You know it's coming but can do nothing to stop it) and we successfully completed the course.

Bridge Over Troubled Water

My first day as an operational dog handler was to prove interesting within minutes of the start of my shift. A call came in to say that a road accident had occurred under Clifton Suspension Bridge on the Portway, and three people had run from a vehicle towards Bridge Valley Road. I arrived within five minutes, located the car, began tracking with Jason and, within one hundred yards located three men hiding in bushes in a copse beneath the bridge. I detained them and they were handed over to local police units. As I was about to walk back to my van the sound of people shouting and clapping drew my attention up to the bridge, where about fifty people lined the edge applauding me.

I felt like John Wayne, what a buzz.

Scaffold

Not long after, I was on foot patrol in the Broadmead shopping area of Bristol when a call came in to say that two men, one carrying a large Adidas sports bag, were hooking clothing through the letter box of a well known menswear shop. Apparently one of them using a long hooked rod had pulled a rail of clothing towards the door where they proceeded to pull the clothing, shirts, trousers etc. through the fairly large letter box. Quite ingenious. They then packed what they could into the very large holdall and ran away from the scene. I quickly returned to my van and drove to where they had been last seen, and saw both men running down the road still carrying the bag. When they spotted me they separated and one ran towards a very dark side street, hotly pursued by my dog Jason, who had seen him run and without any instruction from me, jumped out of the window and ran after him disappearing from my view with the sound of his claws scratching on the road as he skidded and picked up speed. I jumped out of the van and ran towards the last sighting and turned a corner to find pedestrians and parents with pushchairs, all looking towards the suspect, about eight feet up some scaffolding with Jason hanging from his coat collar and feet off the ground like a large bat. I lifted the dog off and arrested the man on suspicion of burglary but he was shaking so much I had great difficulty getting the handcuffs on. When I marched him back, two members of the public were guarding my van with the doors wide open and the keys in the ignition (there are some good guys in this world), but I had learnt a lesson and afterwards, always removed the keys.

Pleased That She Ducked

One very rainy cold night in November I had occasion to drive off my area into Headquarters to pick up some paperwork. On my way back I picked up a radio message to say that an attempted robbery had occurred near the M32 motorway. By chance, I had just turned onto the motorway and saw an AA van with a vehicle that had broken down and standing beside was the patrol-man and a female driver. I was the first police officer to arrive and heard that a man in dark clothing had approached them carrying a gun, and tried to rob the woman, but ran off when the AA patrol-man intervened. He described the weapon as a revolver with a short lanyard type rope attached to the butt, resembling a military service type gun.

This had only just happened so I drove around to search the area near the centre of Bristol and after a few minutes, in the dull yellow glow of the street lights, I saw a slim dark haired man standing in the doorway of a building. It was a typical, dismal, damp November night but through my open window I could see clearly, that from the edge of his coat sleeve he had a revolver in his right hand with a rope lanyard hanging from it. I knew I had the right man so called up on the radio to let everyone know that I had located this person, and requested backup. When a dog handler calls for back-up it means there's a real problem. I turned the vehicle round and drove back again to get another look, but he left the doorway and walked past me along the pavement. I had to stop him and intended to get the dog out from inside the van but, annoyingly, the cage door jammed. I jumped out and ran around to open the rear doors, momentarily more vulnerable, turning my back towards the suspect. Jason needed no encouragement and had eyes on the suspect as he leapt to the ground. Looking over my shoulder I turned to watch the man appear in the middle of the road about twenty five yards away. He stood squarely with feet apart and both arms straight out holding the pistol aimed directly at me. An ominous click sounded as he cocked the gun and shouted

"You're dead you bastard."

He fired it as I ducked and released Police Dog Jason who ran and launched straight into his chest, taking him down to the ground. I joined them and after a struggle managed to pull the lanyard down his arm yanked the gun away and threw it out of reach, with sparks flying as it bounced down the road. With the help of some other officers (who unfortunately were also nipped by the dog), the man was overpowered and arrested.

We regularly train for gun attack and Jason performed as if it was an exercise but with a little extra adrenaline. He settled back into the van to sleep, with one eye open, whilst I went into a station to start writing, but a senior officer told me to go and get a drink first. Other officers had witnessed the event from their vehicles and could hardly believe what had happened, and a Detective with the female complainant had parked further along the road and were so fearful that they had hidden down behind the dash. The gun turned out to be a replica Smith and Wesson 38 with drilled out barrel, which held one real bullet in the chamber that fortunately failed to fire.

The man went to court and was subject of a mental health order and remanded in custody.

For our actions, Jason and I received commendations from the Crown Court Judge and the Chief Constable.

Another one of my nine lives. John Wayne lives on.

Misper

Reports came in of a missing vulnerable, suicidal man who had gone missing in a village on the outskirts of Bath. Due to the local dog handler being on leave I was sent there to assist. When I arrived I was met by his concerned family and friends who told me that he had left a suicide note and was in possession of tablets and a bottle of whisky. There had been a recent siting of him near the edge of a large field which was surrounded by hedges with deep undergrowth and woods on the far side. Police dog Jason quickly picked up track and began moving toward the centre of the field in a straight line. After about one hundred yards he went into 'the down' indicating to me that he had located an object with human scent.

He had found a Golden Virginia tobacco tin containing some tobacco, roller and cigarette papers. A family member who had accompanied me confirmed that it was similar in every respect to his missing relative's property. Continuing tracking we reached the large wooded area and Jason dived into the undergrowth and began to bark vigorously, indicating the presence of a person. In the long grass I could see a man lying on his back and his identity was confirmed by the relative. There was no response from him and lying nearby were three pill bottles and an empty whisky bottle. An ambulance arrived and the crew joined me, together with a Police Sergeant, so, thinking my work was done I started walking back towards my van. What happened next was unbelievable as the man who had appeared unconscious jumped up and punched the Sergeant breaking his nose. Presumably aggressive, due to finding his suicide attempt thwarted, he was eventually overpowered, arrested and taken to Bath Hospital.

Jason Car Thief Retrieve

The details of several stolen cars had been circulated via the police radio and driving through Yate in North Bristol, I realised I was right behind one. I opened the dog cage door so that Jason could be deployed out of the drivers window, as we trained for many times. The solo Ford driver knew straight away that I was behind him and after a short car chase the car skidded to a halt, the driver abandoned the vehicle and ran off. Jason jumped out the window after him, and the car thief managed to climb a wall and then onto a garage roof. As I climbed the wall he saw me and jumped down into a lane and ran, but his journey was short lived as Jason was after him.

I heard a shout..."Oh God, no..please get him off"

With that, the dog appeared and was actually retrieving the car thief by dragging him along the road back to me. Brilliant! The car thief was very relieved when he saw me and the dog released his grip when I called, and back at the station the torn arm received treatment from the police Doctor.

Sending police dogs out of the window of a police van was proving to be very successful with another car recovered and villain in custody. Well done Jason. What a good boy.

Butt Of The Joke

At Whitchurch airfield in South Bristol there had been an unlawful gathering of traveller's caravans with various vans and trucks, most of which were untaxed and uninsured. Bristol Council had obtained a court order for their removal from this site. There was always aggravation during these events and police were normally in attendance throughout proceedings to prevent a possible breach of the peace. Sure enough I was dispatched to assist the local officers with Police dog Jason, and on arrival I was directed to an area where several council trucks had been damaged by stones thrown through the side windows. A worker said he had just seen someone running from the trucks toward some waste ground nearby, so I began searching the open ground with Jason off the lead, and he quickly disappeared into some undergrowth. Almost immediately I heard a bark followed by a very loud blood curdling scream.."Help Heeeelp... Get him off"

I ran into the bushes and saw a man squatting down with his trousers around his ankles. Jason then pulled the man over and dragged him by the trousers across the ground with him ending up lying flat on his back. That was an unusual but effective retrieve! I called the dog out and Jason continued to watch whilst I questioned the man. Unfortunately it wasn't the culprit as we had presumed, but a council truck driver and it really wasn't his day. He had been called at short notice to cover for a colleague but was feeling a bit under the weather himself and really should not have been there at all. There were attempts to negotiate with the travellers when stones began to fly and he had run to move his truck, and jumped into the cab to find his seat full of broken glass. Needing somewhere quiet to remove pieces of glass from his buttocks he had furtively taken cover, only to be dragged out by a great big dog. I apologised and made the peace with him and as Jason had not injured him, no complaint was made. I often wondered if the original informant knew it was his mate in hiding and literally stitched him up. We will never know, but they certainly had a laugh about it.

Dog Section Sally

Progressed To Second Dog Sally Explosives

Jason was my first working police dog when demand arose for more 'explosives' search dogs, but German Shepherds are big animals to fit into small spaces and Spaniels were to be trained, so I acquired a Springer called Sally. Training was fascinating as we learned how and where devices had been detonated previously. Most notably the 1984 Brighton Hotel bombing of Prime Minister Margaret Thatcher and her Cabinet Members, and the car bomb in 1979, which killed Shadow Secretary of State for Northern Ireland, Airey Neave. Training required high standards of success but at a military base, one dog embarrassed his handler by retrieving a bomb instead of quietly indicating it's position....and failed the course.

Sally passed the assessments and I was then patrolling with two dogs. Whenever VIPs visited our force area, all sites had to be checked and kept secure prior to their arrival. In general, people were asked not to leave bags or parcels unattended. A lunch time call came in from the Dragonara Hotel that a suspect bag had been found in the dining hall and no-one had come forward to claim it. When I arrived, the whole building had been evacuated and a cordon placed at each end of the street to keep everyone at a safe distance. I donned a full Kevlar trauma suit with helmet, visor and boots (which weighed a ton) and slowly approached the restaurant doors with Sally happily beside me on a lead. We entered and found the dining tables full of steaming plates of half-eaten meals. I could see the bag as described and was about to put Sally to search when a man who had somehow got through the cordon, came in behind me. "Officer I left my briefcase here and I'm just coming to collect it" He described the exact location and the suspect bag was indeed his. A siren could be heard getting louder outside. "Do you hear that? It's the Bomb Squad" I said. His forgetfulness had caused an enormous amount of disruption to a lot of people and I'm pretty sure he wouldn't be doing it again.

Photographic Evidence

Identifying suspects can be difficult as most people don't really notice the detail of a person's appearance. A woman had arrived home from holiday and was unpacking her bags when an intruder appeared in her bedroom. As he made to escape she held up her Polaroid camera and took a photograph of him, then he ran out across a road and into a field. In the thirty minutes it took me to arrive, the photo had developed into a clear face so I knew exactly who to search for. The field track led towards an industrial area with fuel and chemical storage facilities, warehouses and railway lines. I could see a figure across the fields about a mile ahead of me and with a strong scent to follow, the dog began to pick up pace and I began to jog, closing the gap quite quickly. When close enough, I shouted for him to stop and he did and then to my surprise, another dog handler appeared from a gateway and approached the suspect as well. I told the suspect why I had stopped him and he denied being at the cottage, until I showed him a rather good photograph. The other dog handler was amused and then stated that he was a British Transport Police officer and had tracked from a train which had been stopped with the emergency communication cord after a serious assault, and the train was still stationary. His track had led to the same suspect, and as GBH was the more severe crime he took the arrest.

Miners Dispute Yorkshire

The strike of 1984/85 was a major industrial action, lead by Arthur Scargill of the National Union of Miners against the Government's National Coal Board. Police were called in to keep the peace and as a consequence of aggression, dog handlers were sent to assist.

It was a very cold December day in late 1984 when another dog handler and I arrived at an old RAF camp called Bawtry which had been a Bomber Command station during WW2. Our job was to guard the nearby coalmine whilst the main police units were resting, and patrol on foot and monitor the site to prevent intruders.

One particular night we were in the main control room where CCTV monitors were being used. I suggested that instead of constantly panning the camera around, it should be focused on our dogs lying in the open back of the van. My dog Jason was always very alert and sure enough after about an hour we saw him sitting up looking towards the outer fence. One of the camera operators panned his camera towards where the dog was looking and zoomed in on three men who were carrying sacks and what appeared to be wire cutters. We watched them come through the fence and start filling their bags. My colleague and I ran to the van got our dogs and ran towards the outer fence where all three were detained. On closer inspection we found that the fence had actually been cut open many times and "stitched"up with a piece of wire so they hadn't actually damaged it, and the sacks contained only slag which they were going to use on their fire at home to keep families warm in freezing weather. They seemed decent desperate chaps, so in view of what we had found apart from trespass, we decided let them go with a strong warning. It was a bad time for the miners and the massive anti-authority local feelings made it challenging for the police trying keep order. I was glad to leave after my seven day duty to make our way back to Bristol, and the overtime came in handy just before Christmas.

Dog Section Rocky

Pretrained Trials Standard Dog Rocky

A colleague, Bob, recommended an expensive hotel to take my wife out to dinner, which I did, and he advised me to live every moment and enjoy the good things that life has to offer.

My dog Jason became ill with a tumour, possibly as a result of drinking contaminated water at the coal mine, and his days were numbered. Bob also became ill and, when it was necessary to hand over his young police dog Rocky, he seemed satisfied that I would be the one to take up Rocky's lead. A testing time all round. Bob was determined to fight his illness and would often say that he wasn't ready to 'be a sunbeam'.

Bob had nurtured Rocky from pup to training age, and colleagues thought that the more gentle obedient young dog would not suit my style of policing, but I bonded with the long haired animal and continued to develop his operational effectiveness. We competed in the internal Avon and Somerset obedience trials, finishing top of the score board. The final day at Kingsweston House had begun cloudy and overcast but as we entered the field to be judged on the final discipline the weather cleared, and a bright sunbeam of light shone through the clouds reflecting on us all.

South West Regional Dog Trials followed, where we succeeded winning the hard surface tracking trophy for one of the most difficult disciplines. The venue was the tarmacced surface of a disused motor racing circuit and the track of 335 paces, laid thirty minutes prior, consisted of eight legs and angled turns culminating with the final article which was a vehicle ignition key. The weather had been cold and wet and a blustery wind meant that any scent could be blown way off track. As I approached the starting point I heard "You'll be lucky! Everyone's failing and it's chucked down with rain since your track was laid." The ground was indeed wet and dotted with large pools of water seven to eight feet wide which Rocky tracked through and onward to find the final key resulting in the top score and the Mary Jordan Trophy.

At one competition, some gun attack tests were scheduled before the stick attacks. The sound of gunshot made all the dogs agitated and when a volunteer, wearing a protective sleeve, emerged with a stick and refused to put it down, Rocky disarmed him with such force that he was knocked to the ground and refused to run for the dog again. Rocky soon earned a reputation for being a reliable working dog with an effective bite.

Policing can be tough but professionally trained dogs and handlers can help to achieve results in securing property and protecting the public. The fact that people choose to run off and not listen when they are told to stop, causes them to be bitten and physically detained. The injuries are an unfortunate by-product with serious consequences to the suspect and to the team responsible. Therefore the dogs were implemented only with justification, and great responsibility.

Playing To Scare Dog

School liaison days allowed primary age pupils a close up view of a police dog, with a chance to pat and climb on his back, and watch demonstrations of sniffing out property and catching 'criminals'. Children often sent in thank you letters with their drawings of Rocky and these proved helpful when I was accused of having a dog 'out of control' !

In the early hours on night patrol I saw a youth using the orange ball of a belisha beacon light shade as a football in the road, and when approached to give some friendly advice he kicked the lamp and ran around a corner. Driving after him I found that he had joined a group of lads blocking the street, and as I parked my van they gathered on one side and began attempting to lift and tip it over, with me still inside. Completely unacceptable behaviour. Then they noticed the dog and scattered. I gave chase on foot and when challenged they didn't stop, so I released Rocky and followed them, finding lads climbing up trees, onto walls and cars and one on the ground with Rocky attached to his arm. On my command, Rocky released his grip, and lay down barking while the young man stood up and I searched him. His mistake was then to kick Rocky in the face and run off again, resulting in an extremely serious leg wound witnessed by another police crew. The young man's version of events, as told to his father, resulted in a complaint investigation where I could have been subject to charges, loss of job and prison. Fortunately that didn't happen and the lad was advised that anyone kicking a police dog should expect to be bitten.

Got It In The Neck

One night shift I chose to park up near a school and wait for the next call. Within a few minutes a burglar alarm sounded, and a man came out of the darkness, jumped the wall by the side of my van and made off across the road. I got Rocky out and challenged the runner to stop or I would release the dog. Foolishly he just kept running and with the dog closing in, he tripped on the kerb, and instead of the intended right arm he was bitten in the neck and brought down with a loud thud. I called the dog out and examined the man who was bleeding profusely from the lower part of his neck and with no response he appeared to be unconscious. A police car arrived and two officers rushed him to Frenchay hospital whilst I returned to the school to find that a lot of damage had been caused with classrooms completely trashed and chairs and tables strewn about. (It turned out that about ten thousand pounds worth of damage had been caused.)

I became increasingly worried about the events of the evening, the possible fatality and repercussions to me and my dog. I drove around for about an hour before being called in to Staple Hill police station to speak to the duty Sergeant. 'Oh hell', I thought 'this is it', my days as a dog handler or even a police officer were numbered. I made my way to the station and walked along a corridor to the custody area. Standing facing me in the room was the Sergeant, and a man who had his back towards me had a large wound dressing on his neck and was the man that my dog had stopped from the school. Well thankfully he is alive!

The sergeant said the man had told him how he got the neck injury 'But how did this happen?' he then lifted the man's shirt, exposing a series of long cuts down the back, deep into his skin. It transpired that as the dog closed on him the claws had made contact with his back causing a further wound and the bite to his neck, which on examination was only one inch away from the carotid artery. He was later charged with criminal damage and made no complaint regarding the bite.

If only he had listened to me and 'Picked The Sensible Decision'.

Pleaded To Send Dog

Police cars were pursuing a suspect stolen vehicle approaching my area at great speed and which finally crashed near a back lane in a residential area of Kingswood, a northern suburb of Bristol. Whilst en-route I heard that the driver had left the scene on foot and when I arrived, the vehicle door was open and a trail of video cassettes and papers lead towards an access lane to rear gardens which were separated by six foot high wooden fences. Rocky was the grand old age of seven with the hard bite of a mature dog, and still operated at speed. On the tracking line he immediately picked up a strong scent and we were away, but then he stopped abruptly by the first back gate. His barking indicated that someone was in the garden, and as I shone my torch I saw a man climb the fence and jump into the next garden along. I ran in and told Rocky to jump the fence and as I followed I caught sight of the man climbing another fence, and then another until at about the fifth fence, several bedroom windows opened. Neighbours concerned about the crashing sounds of two people and a dog jumping fences voiced their concerns and one shouted. "Hey mate let your dog go. Go on your slowing him up."

He was of course right but in the back of my mind I thought that if I could detain him without another bite and complaint that would be preferable. However, after someone else shouted the same thing I thought, ok I have shown restraint in front of several witnesses, but now it was time to challenge and if necessary, release the dog. Rocky went over another fence into the darkness and I heard the sound of someone running and then a blood curdling scream as Rocky detained the man as he had run down a garden path and into the back lane. The suspect had run into the dog in the darkness and was being held by the groin causing him extreme pain. It must have been horrendously painful and not what I wanted to happen under any circumstances.

He was arrested on suspicion of taking the vehicle but it later transpired that he was actually the owner and panicked because he was uninsured. After receiving hospital treatment for a nasty wound near his left testicle another complaint came winging its way in my direction, along with a complaint from a Consultant at the hospital.

The Consultant was on duty on my next set of nights so I arranged to call in and speak with him with Rocky behaving impeccably as I explained the circumstances of both recent bites and also the previous Boxing Night incident which had filled the A and E department. He was satisfied with what I told him and withdrew his complaint but the injured man didn't and it was added to my growing list of complaints.

A senior officer who I knew, was visiting the station and stopped me to say that he had been to the Complaints and Discipline Department. There he had seen the various piles of complaint reports with a couple for one policeman, four or five for a few others and then there was my name with eleven towering files. I asked him if he had read the details of each one and whether he thought I was justified in my actions, and he said yes. (But declined to put that in writing ;)

Bottles of Wine – Case Dismissed

Saturday nights were always busy and I was asked by the control room to keep an eye out at a local night club where trouble was expected. It turned out to be quiet except for the odd idiot who taunted Rocky by looking in the back window of the dog van, but they didn't stay long after the dog started launching himself at the cage door and the van began rocking from side to side.

By 2a.m. most of the club fraternity had made their way home when I was called to an alarm actuation of an off-licence and shop just two streets away. Glad to get away from any more stupid behaviour, I was there in minutes and could see the smashed shop window with glass everywhere. There was a display of wines and spirits with several gaps where, I presumed, bottles had been removed.

Because of the broken glass I had to be careful that the dog didn't step on it, so decided to start a track ten yards passed the shop front and he immediately picked up a scent and was away. Fresh scent meant a good chance of getting a result, and with no-one in sight, the dog tracked along at least five streets before suddenly leaving the pavement and pulling me up a narrow path into a front garden of a residential property. He dived into a large bush and began barking, and immediately a voice shouted "Ok.Ok don't let him bite me"

I shouted "Police dog come out with your hands up now"

I called the dog out and shone my torch into the hedge where a youth lay on his back near two wine bottles labelled with the name of the shop that had been burgled.

"You've got a good dog there mate, oh hello it's you Jim" he said.

I recognised him as one of my previous clients and replied "We meet again! I would have thought you'd have learnt your lesson by now"

And he said "Just my luck them sending you....shit!"

I arrested him for burglary and the shop owner positively identified the bottles as coming from his shop, so it didn't need Sherlock to work that one out, and he was also charged with £1000 worth of damage to the window.

I was glad that on this non-aggressive occasion there was no dog bite or complaint to answer for, and it all seemed straight forward with an admission of guilt at the scene and also by statement when interviewed by CID. However, about four weeks later I happened to bump into the detective who had dealt with the prosecution and I was stunned to hear that at the court hearing the job had been kicked out. The defendant had changed his plea to 'not guilty' and as physical evidence was missing, of glass particles from his clothing and glass samples from the scene, they aquitted him of all the charges. It was really frustrating as I believed I had enough evidence, bearing in mind I had tracked him from the premises and didn't just stumble upon him by chance. I'm sure I could have convinced the court of this man's guilt but as a guilty plea was expected I had not attended court.

Public Thank Search Duo

At around lunchtime, money was being delivered by secure van to a public house on a busy roundabout. A motorcycle pulled up near the money transfer and the pillion passenger approached the van, pointed a gun at the security officer and demanded the money. The security officer threw the money and himself into the van and closed the door, then sounded an alarm which sent the man back to his motorcycle to make an escape, closely pursued by a Traffic Police car that happened to be close by. After a chase of about seven miles the motorcyclist lost control and dropped the bike, then made off across fields, leaving his pillion passenger and a gun to be picked up by the Traffic officers. Believing the suspect was possibly armed, instead of tracking, I used my dog to quarter the field off the lead. Rocky ran up and down barking, and indicated that someone was in the hedge. After putting the dog on the lead, I challenged but there was no reply, so Rocky went in and dragged the suspect out. No gun was found. I handcuffed the man and marched him back to the road where interested locals had gathered and stood applauding our success.

Irretrievable Exercise

One of the things we trained our dogs to do was to find hidden objects in long grass or undergrowth. The idea was to locate heavy objects which the dog was unable to lift or carry such as a heavy bar or money safe. A 56 pound weight was used for this purpose. The object was handled so applying human scent, then hidden in long grass and the dog sent in to find it. Once the dog located it they were encouraged to bark, alerting the handler, and saving valuable time and resources by covering large areas quickly.

There had a been a large number of burglaries, mainly around the North Bristol area, where safes had been removed from premises. One safe was thought to have been dumped on a section of verge of the M5 Motorway North of Bristol, and I was tasked with searching several miles to find it. This information had come from a person who had been arrested so a bit vague as to exactly where. After several miles the dog disappeared into some long grass by the post and rail livestock fence, and soon began barking. He had located a large safe that seemed to be still locked and contents secure.

Nice one Rocky!

Man On Roof

Called to a Rolls Royce dealership in Central Bristol, a person had broken into the premises and damaged at least eight Rolls Royce motor cars by trying unsuccessfully to remove the radios by levering with a bar or screwdriver. The damage to the walnut dash was immense as you would imagine. The key holder who happened to be the owner was seriously upset by the sight of these wonderful cars with thousands of pounds of damage, but no radios had been removed and it was believed that the burglar had been disturbed and was still hiding on the premises. I began searching with Rocky.

Most of the damaged cars were parked on the second floor which also had a mezzanine upper floor. It was an odd building in that a ramp accessed an open air car park where most of the cars were stored.

I started at the ground floor and released the dog to search. He ran through all the floors but quickly ran to the open air car park and began sniffing around a metal drain pipe attached to the additional building on the roof. He persisted to show interest in the pipe and after a short time began biting it and then started barking.

Now that's interesting I thought, why is he doing an irretrievable indication on the base of this fifteen foot drain pipe. Then it dawned on me the burglar must have climbed or attempted to climb up it. I was joined by several local officers including an inspector who looked in disbelief when I assured him that the burglar had climbed up.

He said he was not prepared to send anyone up the drainpipe and how sure was I about this. Having spent almost ten years in the fire service and had been stationed in the Fire Station across the road, I suggested calling out the brigade, and requesting a hydraulic platform. That way if anyone is up there they can be brought down safely as its designed to carry four people and is easy to get into. The Brigade were with us within three minutes as I expected.

During my time as a fireman I was a fully qualified Hydraulic Platform operator so I knew what to expect when I heard the machine operating from the street below but, due to my location, was unable to see it. A powerful searchlight lit up the roof and a police Sergeant and Constable found a man hiding behind a water tank right above where my dog had indicated the drain pipe. He was arrested and brought down and the Avon Fire service thanked for their assistance....(gosh how I wished I was a fireman then). Rocky was praised by all and the Inspector admitted he'd doubted the dog's ability to locate someone at least twenty feet away up on a roof.

Rocky Video

One dark late turn (2pm-10pm) evening I was sent to call that a man had been seen climbing through a house window in Staple Hill. As I arrived, a man carrying a 'swag bag' climbed out of window and ran across a garden. He tried to reach the safety of a bush but as he bent down Police Dog Rocky caught him by the buttocks. Pain caused his right hand to clench which crushed a recently stolen, solid silver snuff box. Found in his jacket was a stolen video cassette of the film 'Rocky', which caused great hilarity back at the station, as did the attendance of Dr Payne who gave him a jab and stitched the wound. The thief was charged with six burglaries and remanded in custody.

Another good job!

Reliant Robin

A call from the M5 motorway reported a collision between an articulated lorry and a yellow Reliant Robin van and the control staff at Almondsbury could hardly contain their laughter when they spoke to me on the radio. The Reliant Robin is a three wheeled vehicle made of fibreglass with one wheel at the front and a motorcycle engine. Made famous by Delboy and Rodney Trotter in the 'Only Fools and Horses' television comedy.

The Reliant driver had failed to stop after hitting the lorry, and had made off towards the M4/M5 interchange. I decided to turn down the M4 towards the Severn bridge and after about a mile found the Reliant on the nearside carriageway positioned facing up the embankment with its single headlight lighting up the night sky. The near-side door was open and a trail of cigarette packets led up the embankment.

I got Rocky out of my van and placed him in his tracking harness. He pulled hard and started tracking up the slope about twenty five yards to the top, and then out of my sight for a moment I felt the line go slack so I knew he had reached the livestock fence. On reaching Rocky I shone my torch and saw his tail wagging and heard a voice say "Good dog there's a good dog" A man was lying on his back with Rocky standing over, staring directly into his face.

I said "Watcha got then" Rocky turned with a look that said 'We never trained for this Dad' Then turned back and nipped him in the hand. The suspect gave out a loud cry and in a Liverpool accent said "Why did he do that, I love dogs " and I jokingly said "Sorry mate he just hates Scousers"

He was arrested by the original traffic officers and later charged with a string of offences, stating that he wished to make no complaint about the dog bite. He was a real old fashioned villain who probably went on to boast about his encounter with my furry friend. On the wall of the cell block he would have seen a photograph of Police dog Rocky entitled 'Crime is a disease... Meet the cure!'

Incident On The Button

An alarm had actuated at a social club on the outskirts of North Bristol and Control confirmed that there were no other units available to attend and I was on my own. I thought 'No problem, there's nothing we can't deal with'.

It makes it easier for a dog handler to operate if nobody walks about leaving false trails which could confuse the dog and delay finding the right track, so the fact that we were first on the scene was good. I found that the premises had been entered by forcing the rear door, and it backed on to fields so we began tracking and quickly picked up a scent moving speedily towards the centre of a large fifty acre field. In the distance I could see the main road street lights. The grass was very long and wet due to recent rain and when I reached roughly the centre of the field the dog went into the 'down' which indicated to me that he had located something bearing human scent. I shone my torch onto his mouth but couldn't see anything, but he had never let me down in the past, so I prised open his jaws and on the end of his tongue was a small pearl shirt button. I put the button in my pocket and carried on tracking towards the main road where I could now see the blue flashing lights of a Police car.

The officer had been talking a man on the grass verge, but saw no reason to detain him until I arrived with Rocky.

The man's jeans were wet from the knees down as were my trousers. When I pointed this out to him I noticed that his top shirt button was missing and the remaining ones looked similar to the one I had in my pocket. He said that the button had been missing for some time and that his mother had forgotten to sew it back on before he went out. ('A likely story!)

When I produced the button from my pocket and told him how I'd come by it, his jaw dropped. He was duly arrested on suspicion of burglary at the social club and later charged and admitted the offence. Admission of guilt due to my evidence brought a satisfactory conclusion, on the button!

Put The Samurai Down

There are many night clubs in central Bristol and though the majority are no problem, one venue in particular was always bad news, however, this was the first time I had been called there with Rocky as it was not my area but my colleague was otherwise engaged.

"Victor Delta can you make your way to central Bristol, officers are calling for assistance. A man is armed with a Samurai sword and is holding police at bay"

This is going to be interesting I thought, but we're trained for it.

After a fast drive across Bristol I arrived at the scene where at least a hundred people were milling around watching the spectacle. Several police carrying long riot shields were talking to a very large individual who was shouting abuse at them and brandishing a samurai sword. The city lights reflected from his skin and from the blade as he kept them at bay, lashing out and striking the police shields. Rocky picked up on the situation and was already wired for action as he jumped out of the van and I thought 'Rocky lad, you and I could be chopped up in little pieces here'

As I approached I shouted very loudly "Police dog, put the weapon down now! If you don't put it down you will end up in the hospital down the road" Although I knew that it could just as easily be my own fate.

He turned and looked at me and I noted fear in his eyes, then almost in slow motion and to my great surprise, he dropped the sword. The crowd gasped.

He followed my orders to "Get on your knees " "Right now on your belly and don't move or I will use the dog", and with Rocky now inches away from his face he began to shake violently and he was handcuffed. He wasn't going anywhere except the cells.

I was thanked by the duty inspector for my valuable assistance in dealing with the life threatening situation without injury to the prisoner or members of the public. Neither of us could initially understand why he gave up so readily when confronted by the dog, but the prisoner later explained that as a young boy a German Shepherd had bitten his right ear clean off, and only with skillful surgery was it fixed back on. (Thinking of my brother, I knew only too well how traumatic that injury would have been.) As a result he was scared of this type of dog and stated that if I had turned up with a Rottweiler or Doberman he would have chopped me up into small pieces. Hmmm well we will never know. Another John Wayne moment.

Dog Loving Drunk

Waiting for the keyholder at an alarm call in Park Street, I stood chatting to a couple of policemen with Rocky sitting quietly, when a drunk lurched up and sat down on the kerb. He said how much he liked dogs and could he pat the German Shepherd. My colleagues were familiar with Rocky and his reputation, and were shocked when I agreed and watched as my dog was cuddled. As he walked away the drunk questioned whether it was in fact a police dog. So I asked Rocky to 'speak' and the drunk moved so quickly he ended up in a heap on the pavement.

Taking The Pee

Sometimes I was called to the City of Bath about nine miles from Bristol to assist if their dog handler was busy or on leave. One evening I was called to help two local police officers struggling to arrest a well known drug dealer standing at the top of a very high staircase, in a row of terraced houses opposite Abbey Churchyards in the centre of the city. I parked my dog van around the corner in front of a marked police car, opposite a taxi rank where several taxi drivers looking in my direction obviously wondering what was going on. Because I didn't think that I needed Rocky, I left him with the cage open so that he could protect the van and access the front of cab whilst I dealt with the job.

We managed to arrest the man, and whilst struggling to apply handcuffs on the pavement outside, a passer-by said that someone was trying to break into my van. I laughed and said that my friend in the van would not allow that to happen, but thanked him and he went on his way.

The two officers thanked me for my help and I ran straight to my van where I found Rocky in the driver's seat looking out of the door which was on the first catch but not fully closed. I heard laughter and shouting coming from the taxi rank and several of them walked over to me. They said that a skinhead with a white teeshirt had tried the door of the police car and found it locked so went to my van. He opened the drivers door, looked around, unzipped his fly, and appeared to be about to urinate on my seat, when a dog that looked as big as a fully grown lion grabbed him by the chest and tried to pull him into the van. As his shirt ripped he head butted the door, closing it and preventing the dog from getting out. He screamed and they saw a lot blood on his shirt as he ran into the road and began running away from the scene towards the city centre, screaming all the way...poor man!!! Being concerned for his well-being(not), I reported immediately to the control room and asked them to circulate his description to all units in the area and to contact the local hospital in case he turned up there. I then left Bath and returned to my patch in Bristol, having given the control room staff a good chuckle. Nothing more was heard of this person.

Doggy Paddle

Called to an intruder disturbed next to a riverside premises.

It was quite a long "haul" driving from the western side of Bristol to this call which began as a foot chase following a burglary where the perpetrator had been disturbed by police. I made my way to the river bank where he had last been seen, and suddenly a man came running out of a side lane and ran along the river bank at high speed.

Believing this to be the burglar as the description seemed to fit, I shouted "Stop, Police Dog" . There was no acknowledgement from him so I released Rocky into a full chase and attack. As the dog closed on him the man dived straight into the river and began swimming "doggy paddle" across the river towards the opposite bank. Rocky went straight in after him and his doggy paddle was faster, I wonder why!?

Then I was worried. Rocky was gaining on him and I considered having to join them if the dog grabbed him mid-river. Hell! it was February and very cold.

The suspect made the far bank a few yards ahead of the dog and began a very slow jog. After about twenty feet he was nailed by Rocky who didn't even bother to shake himself on exiting the water and just pressed home his attack.

Fortunately there was a nearby footbridge and when I reached them, the man was motionless and made no attempt to struggle with the dog firmly attached to his very wet and bedraggled right arm.

He was arrested, admitted the burglary, and received treatment for his injury at Bath Hospital.

Well done partner.

Suicide Is Painless?

Another call reported that a male youth had hung himself in the garage of a family home on the outskirts of Yate, a suburb in North Bristol. It had been reported by a father who had come home after a night out and found his son hanging by short rope from the rafters in the garage. I just happened to be only two streets away so after informing the local control room I made my way, thinking first aid, compassion, suspicious death? On my arrival at the house it appeared to be in darkness except for a dim light which I could see through the glass front door. I saw movement so starting knocking on the door, and shouted "Police" I turned to look at my van and saw Rocky looking at me and he appeared agitated which was not like him at all.

As I turned around to face the door it quickly opened and a person hit me with a baseball bat across the left shoulder. Instead of jumping back I moved towards him so close he was unable to make another hit. I punched him and we both fell into the hallway where a violent struggle ensued. He grabbed my radio and threw it across the hall. He was a big lad about 6ft 6" and as we struggled I managed to keep him down, gradually dragged him towards my radio and I called for assistance. I thought, it could not get any worse than this, but how wrong could I be.

Still pinning him down I looked up and saw his father just standing three feet away holding a large carving knife in one hand and a rope in the other. I told him to dial 999 and tell them I needed urgent help. Things then went from very bad to worse when he dropped the knife right in front of his son who, though still pinned down, grabbed the knife. I was now in serious trouble, so with all the strength I could muster I managed to force his wrist back and pull the knife from his grasp. I threw it into the kitchen just missing his father and the blade stuck into a cupboard where it remained, twanging. At that point I could hear police cars approaching and I knew if the door was closed they would kick the door in. I managed to pull this man across the floor once more as the shocked father opened the door, allowing four police officers in. The son was overpowered but it took all five of us to get him into a police car. He was then conveyed to the local police station where he was detained and later put before the court.

The father later said that his son was upset at being cut down and, when told that the police were on their way to help, declared that he would kill the first officer to arrive.

Why he didn't tell the emergency call operator this I really don't know. I would have certainly used my dog who is trained to deal with violent people who are armed with any type of weapon. Because of the blow I had received from being struck by the bat I attended Frenchay Hospital and received treatment for a badly bruised shoulder. I hoped I would never have one of those jobs again....But...

Two Knives

A similar call had a man under the influence of drugs, armed with two knives and holding his father hostage in a small room. The officers attending had begun to arm themselves with shields but as space was tight, they were impractical and so thinking he would give up, they threatened the man with calling in a police dog, but that had the opposite effect. I arrived and left

Rocky in 'the down' outside while I approached the doorway to assess the situation. The man looked at me and when he learnt that I was the doghandler he brandished both knives and said "Get your dog and I will kill you both" So returning with Rocky, I drew my truncheon and as we both launched into the man he moved forward, so my strike hit him on the head causing a split which sprayed blood onto the ceiling. My truncheon flew into the air and fell behind a freezer. Despite Rocky's grip, the man held on to the knives, and other officers came in to remove them, getting cuts to their hands in the process. At the station the (still high) man had medical attention to his head, but later was found head-butting the cell door, reopening the wound.

About six months later, a similar call to the same address was attended by the same officers. This time the man stood in his garden holding weapons, but when I arrived in the dog van, he threw down the knives and submitted, having learnt one lesson!

Traffic Dog

In the northern suburbs of Bristol sometimes up to twenty cars per night were stolen. The people who stole these vehicles are often called "Joy Riders" It didn't bring much joy to owners of these cars as often they were recovered damaged or never seen again. This was becoming a big problem and steps were being taken by senior officers to "Nip this in the bud" Somebody on the traffic department came up with the idea of a double crewed patrol car with a police dog and handler in the back. The idea being if there was a car chase and the perpetrators bailed out then the dog would give them a nasty surprise should they run off. I arrived for night duty and was told that I was going to ride with my dog in the back of a traffic car. I wasn't too impressed initially, then the thought of a car thief getting a nasty shock from Rocky appealed to my sense of humour.

So I introduced my dog to the crew and put the him on the back seat. We all then went into the station to be briefed about the night's targets and how we were going to use the dog. I emphasised that the crew needed to not get in my way if there was a runner and stay in their vehicle. They all knew Rocky's 'Modus operandi (M.O.) So no problem there.

At the end of the briefing I heard a shout, and my dog barking in the yard below. I ran down fast to see my colleague looking into his patrol car in which Rocky had assumed ownership and was in guard mode so would not let him in. The officer seemed overly annoyed and then explained that his lunchbox was in the car and Rocky had eaten his sandwiches! I apologised and offered him my meal instead.

With no driving to do, I just sat back with Rocky waiting for some action, but not for long. As we stopped at some traffic lights a car pulled up alongside. The passenger wound the window down and said that they had just stolen the car they were in, then made off at speed. Right I thought, now this is going to be interesting. After a pursuit at high speed the car turned into a side street and there was a cloud of blue smoke from tyres as it came to a sudden stop. The driver jumped out and began running but only made about ten feet before he was stopped by Rocky. The traffic officers saw we'd caught the driver, and they searched nearby gardens, finding the man who had previously taunted us. Word got around the area that all Police traffic cars had Police dogs in the back, and not one car was stolen for the entire week of nights. Positive policing.

Broken Neck

There were numerous reports of burglaries where a person seen running away, had mysteriously looked like an astronaut with a big head. Officers in a patrol car passing a garage forecourt noticed a ladder leaning against the building with a man at the top drilling into an alarm box, and armed with the means to disable the alarm. He ran off across a field, pursued by one officer as the other called for back up. I was not far away and soon joined the foot pursuit with Rocky. I caught up with them, grappling in a rhine of shallow water, but every time the officer tried to release his headlock grip, the felon bit him. On my count of three he rolled away and the man crawled out of the ditch and stood up, but quickly pulled out a commando knife, which he held dagger style at shoulder height. Refusing to put down the weapon and ignoring my warning, he was knocked back as Rocky launched at him, leaving a bloody wound. Arrested and taken to hospital for the dog bite, the man was found unexpectedly, to also have a broken neck. The man's address was searched and stolen property recovered along with a metal support cage designed to support a patient's head and neck when injured. The neck fracture obviously existed before and the man had removed the support prior to this evening. Previously, when covered by a stretchy balaclava hat, the wearer would have resembled an alien or astronaut, thus solving the mystery.

Dog Section Drugs

Glastonbury

Rocky had also been trained to seek out controlled drugs, and dogs were proving to be effective. I was deployed at a checkpoint near to the Glastonbury festival at Worthy Farm, to stop and search suspect vehicles. Information had been received that a white transit van containing large quantities of drugs had slipped through the net and had got onto the site, much to the frustration of the police on the ground. The plan was to detain the vehicle on its exit and do a thorough search on the of chance that something may still be in the vehicle and detectible. A tall order I thought at the time but worth a shot as I had an excellent drugs search dog.

The information from West Midlands Police was that the van had left Birmingham loaded with cannabis and possibly other drugs too. The van turned up at my location and was ordered to stop, though I wished I'd stopped him on the way in. The driver was an African Caribbean man 6ft 6" tall wearing a white suit and white Stetson cowboy hat. I was greeted with a big smile and "What can I do for you Officer" I told him the reason why he'd been stopped and he was very compliant and couldn't have been more friendly...but I didn't feel friendly.

I opened the back of the transit van and I was knocked down by the smell of cannabis, you didn't need a dog, it was overpowering, but the van was completely empty. I closed the doors and made my way to the front cab of the vehicle. The driver was standing by the drivers door still grinning and asking if he could go on his way. I told him that he wasn't going anywhere until I searched the cab area. He still continued to smile at me and seemed quite a nice bloke and I was sort of warming to this man with a Brummey accent.

At the time police dogs did not have to generally wear collars, and when I placed a leather collar over the Rocky's head, it was his indication to 'search for drugs'. I opened the cab door with this gentleman watching, and the dog immediately indicated drugs in the seat adjustment channel where I found a concealed single wrap of cannabis. He was no longer smiling when the four thousand pounds cash found in his pockets was confiscated, and he was sent to the Magistrates Court nearby.

Professionally Trained Spliffer Dog, What A Shower

I had only a few opportunities to use Rocky for drug searching but on this particular occasion it became quite interesting.

A large country house was the subject of a full scale drug search and Rocky and I were to assist the local drug squad. After they had done their bit, I placed a collar on the dog which instructed him to search for drugs rather than a person. The property was set in three acres of grounds, and having searched several outbuildings we moved in to the large eight bedroomed house. The ground floor revealed nothing, although he did indicate a sideboard drawer where drugs had been found earlier by the squad, and that showed me that he was searching correctly. The drugs squad had already found enough drugs to arrest the occupants of the house and I was doing a final sweep. Each of the bedrooms had beautifully tiled en-suite shower and bathrooms which were huge by normal standards. I reached the last of the eight bedrooms and up until then had no indication from the dog, when suddenly he started scratching the the shower outlet drain, giving me a positive indication,

The drain cover was quite large so I called Rocky back and began to lift it but, as quick as a flash,

Rocky put his nose down the drain and began devouring whatever was down there.

Oh hell he's never done that before! I prised open his jaws and he eventually allowed me to look inside. If he has swallowed a controlled substance this could be fatal.

I was relieved when I recognised a strong smell of cannabis on his breath, but didn't know what amount he'd eaten or whether it could be harmful. I wasn't going to take any chances and, slightly embarrassed at admitting Rocky had eaten the evidence, I told the sergeant in charge what had happened and returned urgently to the station to seek advice.

On that journey I glanced into the rear view mirror and saw that his eyes looked glazed and he seemed very relaxed with a sort of calmness about him.

When I got back I called the veterinary hospital and they said that he was in no danger but advised to just go off duty and make sure he didn't work for twenty four hours. By the time I reached home the dog was fast asleep so I carried him from the van into the kennel where he remained till the next morning. The next day he was no worse for wear, and fortunately I was on leave for a couple of days so I could keep my eye on him. He was fine....big lesson learnt!

Drug Squad

I'd been called to assist the drugs squad in Bath but I didn't know any of the officers in that department. I entered the hallway of a terraced house and a plain clothed detective told me to go into the lounge and liaise with the officer inside. The room held five long haired, bearded, scruffy men and I had Rocky on the lead, watching them and sitting whilst I prepared to put the collar on that would indicate for him to search. Another man, of similar appearance suddenly ran down the stairs and as he entered the room, Rocky unexpectedly launched at him pinning him down on the staircase but didn't bite him. As I began to apologise, the other men all burst out laughing and I heard "What a clever dog, he knows a bad guy". Of all the men in the house, Rocky had picked out the only one that was not a policeman! He went on to do the search and found a small quantity of a high class drug in microdots, hidden behind the screwed on cover of a light switch. Clever dog indeed!The Court Usher

One night I was called to a builders merchants yard in Staple Hill where two men had been seen climbing over the fence. When I arrived I had a quick look around for any obvious signs of entry but found none. Due to the nasty looking barbed wire fence I decided to wait for the key holder who arrived within minutes and we were in. Like a familiar training exercise, I shouted a warning before releasing the police dog into the darkness to search,

As the dog passed a large timber storage shed he barked, indicating to me that there was someone in side. The lock on the door had been forced so I opened it, challenged again and released the dog into the darkened room. Suddenly there was a crash as Rocky located and bit the right arm of one of the men holding an iron bar ready to hit me or my dog. The pressure of the bite was so strong the man collapsed to the ground and didn't move. Then Rocky suddenly looked around to my right and he leapt and bit the leg of the other man who was about to strike me with a broom handle, and who also fell to the ground injured and incapacitated.

A police task force van arrived with six officers on board and they conveyed the injured burglars to the police station where they were seen by a police doctor and later charged. But for the dogs quick reactions I think I may have been in a bit of trouble. They both pleaded not guilty and I attended Bristol Crown court to give evidence. Whilst I was giving my evidence about how they were armed with weapons the court usher caught my eye. Every time I happened to glance at him he would smile at me and wink. I didn't know him and hadn't seen him before that day. I thought this a bit odd and continued giving my evidence. The judge took a dim view of their actions and gave them both custodial sentences.

After the judge left the court the usher came over and told me that I was on a winner as the Judge was the Honorary Chairman of Battersea dogs home and would have been appalled at someone trying to injure a dog like that, especially a Police dog. ('Never mind me then')

Placed Truncheon Saved Detective

I was on routine patrol one evening when a call came in stating that an officer who was in plain clothes had stopped a vehicle because he believed the driver was under the influence of drink or drugs. He needed a uniform presence and the driver and passenger were making threats towards him. I was not far away and decided to help although it wasn't a "dog job" but within a minute he had called 10-9 which is code for an officer in trouble requiring immediate assistance.

I was there within two minutes and as I pulled up, I saw the officer struggling with two men who seemed to be pushing and shoving and swearing.

Assessing the situation, I jumped out of the van without the dog and approached them. I was a few feet away when the officer was punched to the ground, then the other male began kicking him. I shouted for them to stop but they both continued kicking, and having given plenty of warning, I drew my truncheon and began striking both men to prevent further injury to the officer who by now was writhing in agony. This had the desired effect as both men ceased their onslaught and fell to the ground beside the officer.

Meanwhile the dog van was rocking with Rocky jumping and barking and trying to get out to protect me. If I had used Rocky the men may have sustained more than a bit of bruising. They were both arrested for assaulting a police officer and one for drink driving, and both made a complaint of assault against me.!

I was used to this as a dog handler, but as no dog was used this could be interesting.

A court date was set with both pleading 'not guilty' to all charges. Because they had made a complaint against me, the police were obliged to investigate and in the court were two officers from the police complaints department. This didn't bother me as I had done nothing wrong and was just doing my job protecting another Constable in the execution of his duty, as stated in law.

It got interesting when one of the defendants produced a photograph showing a massive amount of bruising all over his body, and up until that date, the photo had not been produced in evidence either to the defence or prosecution.

I was not happy with this and informed the police solicitor who halted proceedings and called for the charge sheet to be brought to the court from the police station where they had been taken on that night. The injuries recorded were nothing like those shown in the photo which, it transpired, had been sustained at some later incident. With the defendant facing a possible charge of perjury, the photograph was withdrawn.

Bearing in mind the proceedings were monitored by the police complaints department when asked why I had used my truncheon on the defendants the conversation went like this

"I made a mistake there."

"You admit that you made a mistake?

"Yes, Your Worships, I should have hit them sooner."

The court became suddenly quiet.

"Explain that comment officer" said the magistrate

Both complaints department officers looked worried, but I said

"Your Worships, the officer on the ground receiving these blows was off work for some time following this incident. If I had hit them sooner I believe his injuries would have been less severe, that's all I meant."

I looked at the complaints department officers and I think detected a wry smile.

The defendants were both convicted and had custodial sentences and the complaint against me was dropped.

Job done!

Hot Dog For Supper

At 2am I had been dispatched to an alarm at a social club that had been reported by a passer by. I had been to this building many times with false alarms caused by equipment failure, but because it was in the early hours I was expecting it to be a genuine call. Sure enough on my arrival I was met by two local officers at the damaged front door which had been forced, allowing entry into the club.

Rocky made a quick search and I found a rear window which opened out to a large playing field where the burglar had made his escape. Outside there was a bottle of vodka and some cigarettes on the grass beneath the window, and as the job was only twenty minutes old I thought I might get a track away and sure enough off the dog went nose to the ground and pulling well.

The field had a hedge in the centre and then a gate led to a further massive field but on reaching the hedge, the dog disappeared into the very long grass and found a case of vodka and several hundred cigarettes.

Great I thought, and I called up on the radio to inform the other officers of my find, but as I finished my radio message I heard the sound of someone running. It was pitch black so I shone my torch into the field and saw a person running towards the road and I could just pick out his shape in the dim distant streetlight..

I shouted "Police dog stand still or I will send him" but he carried on running.

Rocky needed no encouragement and shot off as soon as he was released and as he approached his quarry the man stopped running, faced me and put his hands in the air. With a perfect stand off

the dog circled him, barking and watching for any further movement. He began shouting at me and I couldn't make out what he was saying so I shouted "Just don't move and he won't touch you"

He began shouting again and as got closer I heard what he was saying.

"Your dog has just eaten my Jack Russell! He was only a pup and I couldn't sleep so I decided to take him out"

I said "My police dog has just tracked you from the social club which has been burgled. I didn't see any other dog so you're talking complete rubbish"

I arrested him on suspicion of burglary and marched him back to the club and as I handed him over to the other officers he started telling them that my dog had eaten his Jack Russell, much to their amusement.

All the stolen property was returned to the club and as the man lived nearby we decided to go to his house to make a further search for any more stolen goods. There were lights on in the house and as we knocked on the door a dog began to bark. A lady opened the door and a Jack Russell ran out into the front garden. My suspect's wife confirmed the dog was her husband's newly purchased pup which he had left at home when he went out earlier.

Sitting in the police car watching proceedings and listening to what was being said, he admitted the burglary and after a search of his house we found more stolen property from other burglaries. He later admitted fifteen other offences which were taken into consideration by the court, and was sentenced to a term of imprisonment.

Police dogs are trained to not attack a person who stops running and shows no aggression. The dogs are trained to circle and bark which is not an easy task for an animal running after someone at about thirty miles an hour, who stops suddenly.

The exercise is called a "Stand-off", a very difficult discipline, sometimes they get it right other times they have been known to pile in. On this occasion the dog got it spot on, but the ones that keep running and don't stop...well that's a different story.

Prisoner Trapped... Sent Down

After a quiet night it was good to get the call to assist two officers attending an alarm call at a large garage in the Redland district of Bristol. From outside, they had shone their torches through a window to see an open safe with it's contents strewn around the office, and from that room there was access to a large repair shop with several cars on hydraulic ramps above inspection pits. They had heard a metallic sound and believed that the burglar was still on the premises, and they directed me to the main door of the workshop which had been forced open allowing access. Rocky was raring to go and I called out "Police dog come out or I will send him in"

In all the years of doing this job I could never understand why people rarely took any notice of that warning to come out and give themselves up. They must have thought they were invisible, but the dogs sense of smell is incredible and so they were going to be found, like it or not.

As usual I didn't get a response and thought 'Ah well here we go again', as I released the dog who shot into the workshop like a rocket. He began prancing around the room with his nose in the air and suddenly began barking beneath a car that was on a hydraulic ramp over a pit. This was a positive indication of a person and, shining my torch down into the pit I saw a man standing there brandishing what appeared to be a large tyre lever or iron bar.

I said "Drop your weapon or I will send the dog down there, drop it now!"

"Send him, I will kill him" he shouted back and began striking the side of the pit with a bar.

I said "Look mate drop the bar and come out or this dog will put you in hospital. come out"

He said.."We will see, send him down here" and again struck the side of the pit.

In the torchlight Rocky launched himself and landed on top of the man who continued to hit out with the bar despite sustaining multiple dog bites and a broken kneecap, but eventually he submitted. I called Rocky out and when I jumped down into the pit to handcuff the man I could see that his clothing was in tatters and he was not in a good way after Rocky had "advised him". An ambulance took him the Bristol Royal Infirmary but if only he had listened to me he would have been fine.

After treatment he was interviewed at Redland Police Station and charged with the burglary. Unbelievably, he had been released from prison that morning after serving five years for safe cracking, but he certainly picked the wrong night and location to return to his line of 'work'.

Well done Rocky, another one bites the dust and back to jail he went, without collecting two hundred pounds! Career criminals seemed to take dog bites as collateral damage and even boasted about about their encounters rather than making complaints which were more likely to come from the yobs.

Latteridge Backtrack

I paraded for duty at Bower Ashton which is the HQ of the mounted and dog section, put my kit and dog in one of the vans allocated to me for my patrol and, as usual, checked the vehicles oil and water, lights etc before going out on patrol. The blue lights worked fine, but when I went to check the two tone horns, the switch had been removed. I looked under the bonnet and the two tone horns had also been removed. I then remembered discussions that the force had deemed dog handlers were unqualified to drive vehicles fitted with them.

I was not happy, especially as I *had* been trained and was authorised to drive to emergencies with the 'blues and two's'. Within minutes of me discovering this I was dispatched to a village on the northern outskirts of Bristol called Latteridge where offenders had run off across fields after burgling a large country house.

At five thirty in the evening the traffic in Bristol is very heavy. I soon got snarled up and made slow progress across the city with just a blue light and headlights on. Motorists did not respond and I seriously cursed the person who authorised the removal of the two tones.

The control room kept calling me for updates on my location as police officers had detained some suspects about a mile away from the burglary and wanted me to search for property, and maybe get a track from them back to the house. Eventually after a long delay and very difficult drive I arrived at the scene and found the officers with two suspects. I began tracking with the dog from them and within one hundred yards Rocky suddenly went to a bush and came out with a pair of good leather gloves. I radioed the officers of my find and continued with the track which by now was one and a half hours old. It was unusual to be tracking in reverse, from suspect to scene, but it was fairly long grass and I had completed tracks twice that old with success. After about a mile I arrived at the house and Rocky led me straight to a window at the back, which had been forced open, allowing entry in the premises. Informed of my positive track, the officers arrested both burglars who were later sent to prison. I gave evidence in this case and after the judge asked me to explain to the jury how police dogs are trained to track, it was accepted that, as an expert witness, my evidence and opinion carried a lot of weight.

I continued cursing the loss of two-tones, but after a lot of complaints and more driver training, they were eventually refitted to the vehicles.

Professionally Trained Soldier Disappears

Staple Hill control room sent me to a remote farmhouse where it had been reported that three men had broken in, one had been detained by the farmers and two had made their escapes.

About a mile from the farmhouse, a man running towards me wearing a string vest and underpants waved as he passed. I thought that he could be one of the burglars trying to make out he was a jogger, cheeky sod. I called up on the radio and by chance another police unit was about a mile behind me and they arrested him, and he was in fact one of the burglars.

I arrived at the farm and was guided to where the third burglar had last been seen. The fields in this area are vast; some several hundred acres and more. I put Rocky to track and he immediately picked up a scent and moved off into a field. It was a very warm July day, and dry weather can sometimes affect the strength of scent left on the ground, but it made no difference to Rocky. We moved across the field at a fast walking pace and soon he went into 'the down'....an unused matchstick, another short distance... a penny coin. Now this is either a police exercise and I've been set up, or this man knows about dog evasion which is normally taught to special forces within the military. I began thinking the latter, and it confirmed my suspicion when the dog tracked and forced his way through a bramble hedge instead of going through the open gateway a few yards further on. Reaching the main railway line, for about a mile we tracked along the track, which is never a comfortable place to be, even when the train drivers are expecting to see you. Frustratingly, by then my radio had failed because of the distance away from the signal-repeater in my van, so I was unable to inform the control of my position and warn approaching trains.

The scent track then went off the rail line towards a large copse, more or less in the centre of a vast field. Very hot and tired, we began moving towards the trees when the dog's head came up, which signalled to me that we were close to our quarry. I decided to remove the tracking harness and "quarter" the woods allowing the dog freedom to search this very dense area. Normally when the dog finds someone hidden they bark and you make your way to their location. The silence was worrying, but Rocky was fearless and had never let me down in the past. I then regretted not continuing with the track, keeping my dog near. Moving quickly into the woods, with relief I saw Rocky's wagging tail and as I called out, he lifted his head and turned with his mouth gripping a large bloodied sweatshirt. It appeared that Rocky had found and bitten his man who had managed to pull the sweatshirt over his head and with undoubted strength caused Rocky to release his bite. The man was nowhere to be seen. The brambles were very thick and high, preventing the dog pressing home his attack. If only I had been there! But as it turned out, it may have saved my life.

I went out of the copse and managed to find a track on the far side, then made my way towards a distant road, eventually reaching tarmac, but there was no further indication of scent.

It took a while to return to the farmhouse and, as I had been out of radio contact for three hours, a Wiltshire Constabulary dog handler was there, preparing to track *me*! Whilst in conversation with the officers at the farm, a call came in to say that a man covered in blood with ripped clothing had been seen in a phone box. It later transpired that an accomplice was waiting with a vehicle nearby and the person I'd been tracking had got away. Later arrested in the Liverpool area, apparently he was a member of Special Forces, absent without leave, who had turned to crime.

I'm glad we did not meet in that wood....

The Policeman's Wife

With a husband working shifts the family routine is never the same from one week to the next and although weekends and evenings can be disrupted, having days off in the week allows for real quality time to be together when places are less busy. In our earlier years together we both worked shifts and had one long weekend a month when we were both off, and that was when his two lovely young daughters usually joined us. His week of nights 10 to 6 coincided with my 3 to 11 late shift so we were like the weather men alternately coming and going. As time went on our routines changed and a decade later we were in a position for me to stay at home to bring up our son.

Having initially trained in the same job as him I understood the effect that shiftwork can have on sleep patterns and tiredness and the seriousness of the work that was hard to switch off from. My Dad had been a policeman and I remember my Mum always being there to listen and support him by creating a happy and orderly home.

Because of the nature of the job, it was sometimes necessary to work on late and not always possible to get a message home. One afternoon I was getting a meal ready when the control room rang to say Jim would be late. I knew the caller and asked him what Jim was up to, was he ok and what time I could expect him home, but he was very vague and couldn't answer any of my questions. But sometimes that's just how it was. I eventually got another call from the following shift control staff to say he'd be home in an hour or two.

Apparently a track had taken him out of the force radio coverage and they had no idea where he was or what had happened to him, other than knowing that the man being tracked was capable of disabling both dog and handler but were unable to pass on that information.

That was food for thought. I knew the job held risk and that his very professional approach with a capable and experienced dog would bring the best possible outcome and I had confidence in Jim's confidence in his dog and his own ability to get the job done. It was as though he was indestructible.

Rolex Watch

One very cold winter's night I was called to a burglary at a remote cottage, about five miles from Bristol, where an elderly couple were distraught. Several family heirlooms had been taken including a Rolex watch belonging to to the lady of the house and which was of great sentimental value.

They had been out for the evening and the burglary could have occurred anytime within five hours.

I went to the rear garden which backed onto open fields, a dog handlers dream, and no one had wandered about so with Rocky being one of the best tracking dogs in the force I had a good chance of some success. Tracking harness on the dog and off we went over the garden wall into the very dark field at quite a fast pace, which told me that the track was more recent than I had originally thought. We kept getting surrounded by cows which are a nuisance if you have a dog but we managed to get through them. After about thirty minutes Rocky went into the down, a quick flash of my torch revealed none other than a ladies Rolex watch. Bingo...the burglar must have dropped it by mistake.... if I got nothing else this was worth a lot in more ways than one.

After more cow evasion I came across a medium sized TV set, which I left to collect later. When a police dog gets near to the person he is tracking his head comes up and this is what Rocky began doing. I came up to a hedge and sitting in there was Mr Burgler, rolling a cigarette and realising that his world was about to change. On my instruction he came out of the hedge with his hands up, I didn't handcuff him but made him carry the television set three miles back to the cottage. It was a pleasure to return the stolen goods including the £5000 watch, to their most appreciative owners. A job well done.

Yate Car Thieves

For a while I lived in a Police House in Yate, where most houses had rear vehicle access with small back gardens, and pedestrian-only footpaths at the front. Cars were often stolen and dumped with the thieves disappearing on familiar footpaths through the estate. My car was a bronze Vauxhall Chevette which I nicknamed "Shove it" as it was a wreck, but an ideal dog carrier between home and station and not the sort that would attract a car thief.

After a very tiring late-turn shift, with the prospect of an early start (quick change over), I was very happy to deposit my dog van at Staple Hill police station and transfer Rocky to my own car along with all my kit, including tracking harness. Getting home at about 11.30pm, I fed the very hungry Rocky and left him to sleep in the kennel that almost filled the back garden.

I was enjoying a welcome cup of tea when I heard Rocky's loud bark, which was really unusual as not even cats bothered him. I ran into the garden and the dog stopped barking but I soon found the cause, as over the fence my car was not where I'd left it. I ran out into the street and checked up to the end of the road where my car was at the junction, under street lights, stationary with both doors wide open. I ran back to the kennel put Rocky into the tracking harness and ran to the car which had been hot wired but had conked out. Later on I found that it had run out of petrol, and I was glad I hadn't stopped to fill up on the way home.

Because the road surface was very damp, any track away from the car was going to be easy peasy for Rocky, and we set off at a very fast pace along the footpath towards Chipping Sodbury. After about one hundred yards he pulled me towards some bushes and began barking.

I shouted "Come on out, Police Dog", and two youths emerged from the bush and were arrested for taking my aptly named 'shove-it'.

They could not believe their bad luck for nicking a police dog handler's car out of all the cars that were available, and that the car seemed to have a mind of it's own and stopped.

Mangotsfield Social Club

I was in the control room at Staple Hill when an alarm call came in to Mangotsfield Social club. In the early hours of the morning, alarm calls were usually caused by a break-in so I didn't hang about and as it was only a short distance away, I was there within five minutes.

As I approached from the front car park I saw a man jump out of the window at the front of the building and he ran past my van and across the road towards a school. Rocky spotted him and was away over my shoulder and out the drivers door window. I lost him to sight momentarily, then heard a thud and a shout coming from the direction of the school playing field. He had caught up with the burgler and had brought him down. The burgler was six foot three and fifteen stone and was stopped in his tracks. Unfortunately he started punching Rocky who retaliated by biting him more than he would have done, resulting in this man pleading with me to call the dog off, which I did.

Other officers took the burglar to hospital immediately to receive treatment for multiple dog bites. I was walking back to my van when the school caretaker opened his window and said that he had witnessed the burglar punching the dog in the face after he had stopped him. He also said that he had heard a strange noise coming from a bush under his bedroom window. I sent Rocky into the bushes where he detained a second man who had been the lookout. Two in hospital, but ah well, all in a good nights work.....interestingly this man will come again.

I was on annual leave when a burglary occurred at a regular target, Bitton Recreation ground social club. Several men were seen to run from the building and one hid in a nearby street. No dog was available but when an officer arrived driving a similar van to the one I used, a man jumped out of a bush in front of several police officers and gave himself up. He thought a dog van had arrived and he was the very same man that Rocky had detained at Mangotsfield three months earlier. He proudly showed officers a newly acquired tattoo which read "Rocky bit me here"

and was Praising This Special Dog. You just could not make this up?

Warehouse Alarm

Weston Super Mare is a coastal town on the Bristol Channel, in the Severn Estuary about twenty two miles south of Bristol, and I was the only dog handler available when an alarm was activated at a large warehouse there. I wasn't very familiar with the area and, without today's satellite navigation maps, it took a while to find the warehouse. Despite it being a large premises only one other officer was available to attend. I decided to place Rocky in the "Down" by one of the doorways while the officer and I checked around the perimeter. There was no sign of a break-in and as the key holder was not available, we decided to resume our patrols, so I quickly joined the M5 Northbound motorway and began heading back to my division. Approaching Avonmouth I went cold and thought something's wrong, something terrible has happened. I turned and looked over my shoulder into the empty dog cage.....oh no I've left Rocky at the back of the warehouse! Hoping that he would still be there, and that I wouldn't get a call, I returned at necessary speed. It seemed much longer than the twenty minutes but I couldn't get there fast enough. I reached the warehouse and ran as fast as I could to find Rocky lying exactly at the point where I had left him forty minutes before. He looked at me as if to say "Where ya been Dad". What a dog, and what a lapse of concentration from an idiot handler! Just goes to show how well trained the dogs were and what a lovely bond existed between Rocky and me. Needless to say that never happened again.

Tytherington Quarry

Late-turn Saturday was always busy and this night was no exception, with the added problem of really thick fog making driving very hazardous and tiring. Just my luck. A motorway traffic car had begun pursuing a stolen pick up truck on the M5 motorway North of Bristol and was heading towards Gloucestershire. This was the furthest point of my area but I started to make my way as, nine times out of ten, the occupants of stolen vehicles baled out at some point of the pursuit. Sure enough after only five minutes I hear my call sign "Victor Delta, start making your way to the M5 near the Glos border, one male person decamped from stolen vehicle" This location was a good eight miles away and in the fog was going to take a while, but I pressed on as fast as poor visibility would safely allow.

On my eventual arrival, the two traffic officers who were with the stolen truck told me that a white male had jumped out of the vehicle and they had chased him but lost sight in the fog. The last sighting was by the livestock fence, that all motorways have, which are post and rail about five feet high with a strand of barbed wire on the top rail. This always makes it difficult for a dog to jump over, so we either placed an arm over the top or threw a jacket over to prevent injury before sending the dog. I sent Rocky over and then placed him in his tracking harness.

Shining my torch into the open field I could barely see five yards. Well I will have trust my dog even more in these conditions. The dog picked up a positive track and we moved at a pace faster than I would have liked but I always went with him whatever. In training we used the command "Seek" to indicate to the dog that you wanted him to track and "Seek On" if there was a break or momenary lull in the track. Rocky was pulling well on the tracking line as the scent was very fresh in the long damp grass helped by the heavy foggy moisture in the air. Athough difficult for me, it was perfect for the dog. I had built a massive respect for Rocky over the years and would trust him with my life. I could not see him at the end of the fifteen foot tracking line but could feel every turn and pull. Suddenly the line went slack and I approached the stationary dog. Instead of just standing still I would have expected him to be in 'the down' indicating that he had found some property or person. I told him to seek on but he didn't move, then repeated the command and still he didn't move. This was ridiculous as he'd never refused a command. I stepped forward to check the problem, and found that we were six inches away from possible disaster. His front paws were literally on the edge of a fifty foot sheer drop. The dog had the sense to not go any further, and saved us both, as we had arrived at Tytherington Quarry,...but where was the driver of the stolen truck? A shout for help came from the man who had fallen over the edge and landed about fifty feet down on a spiral service road, which had saved him from falling even further down the two hundred foot drop. An ambulance was able to reach him easily and he luckily survived with two broken legs.

Thanks Rocky, you are a star.

Praising This Special Dog

A working dog has to be in prime health to keep up the level of stamina. Eight years is a lifetime for a German Shepherd and Rocky had begun to drag his heels showing symptoms of damage to the spine. He had been with me through thick and thin and saved my life on numerous occasions not least on that unforgettable Boxing night. A replacement was sought but a young dog takes time to train and there is no substitute for experience. Unfortunately the job doesn't allow for that and starting off at the deep end is par for the course.

Dog Section Pace

On Remand

Based at Staple Hill police station on 'D' division, I lived in a local Police House and often took my much needed refreshment break at home, always monitoring my radio and prepared to leave at a moments notice if called.

The Police van was in the drive with new dog "Pace" ready for the off. Rocky stared at me from the garden almost asking to go with me, and instead of leaving him behind, I decided to put him the adjacent cage in the van with Pace and give him a run out. I was not authorised to use him as he was no longer a police dog.

My radio suddenly crackled into life..Mass break out at a remand centre which was only a few miles away. Without thinking about my extra passenger I jumped in my van, drove at speed and on my arrival I could not believe my eyes; there were about fifty prisoners attempting to climb the security fence. Some had made it to the top and were trying not to get tangled in the razor wire, some were using cutters to break through, it was mayhem, and I was there on my own as other units had not yet arrived.

So I had another John Wayne moment, the film True Grit came to mind.

I got both dogs out and ran up and down challenging anyone who tried to get over or under the long fence. Two barking and snarling dogs deterred them and nobody escaped, but fighting continued within the centre and was dealt with by Prison and Police riot team.

I felt good that I had managed to stop the escape, but that was short lived. My boss saw me on a television news channel using two German Shepherds, one of which was not actually an authorised working police dog! Just my luck. I was given suitable advice and agreed to leave Rocky at home in retirement.

Protection Taken - Serious Danger

A burglar had reportedly been seen in a large wooded area about twenty miles south of Bristol and although this was not my patch there was no one else available, so I was called to attend. The evening light had faded and I didn't know the area or the officers who met me on arrival, but one of them said that the burglar had been lost to sight about an hour ago and gave me a brief discription. With Police dog Pace off the lead, I began the mammoth task of searching a large dark wood for a scent that would have dimished by each passing minute. But there's always a chance and something we trained for so I persisted for about an hour, calling out to Pace to redirect him in quartering the area, but not picking up a positive scent or finding anyone appearing to give themselves up.

Then with a clear signal on my radio, I heard that the suspect had managed to get home and had been arrested. That's okay I thought as I made my way back to my van, we tried our best and we didn't find him because he wasn't there, and at least Pace has had some exercise at the end of our late turn shift. Back at the dirt track there was a police car parked behind my van and two officers wearing body armour were loading short riot shields into the boot. At that time body armour was only worn for incidents involving firearms or explosives so I wondered what else had happened. Only then did I learn that the suspect I had been searching for had previously been seen carrying what appeared to be a double barrelled shotgun! They were as surprised as me to learn that I hadn't been informed of the potential danger and I can't say that I was very happy about it. The job could be challenging enough without swaying the balance in favour of the villain.

The Final Chapter

Collapse On Duty

After a very busy night driving many miles to numerous jobs, a lull in calls allowed me to take a break and park at the rear of a supermarket. I'd been working from 11pm and it was now 4am and my pack of cheese sandwiches were long overdue. It was a clear starry night and would soon be daylight and the sky seemed very bright even though I was surrounded by street lights. After a few minutes I began to feel very light headed and felt that I was going down with something, maybe a cold or flu. The dog was due a comfort break, so I drove to open space near a large factory about a mile away, parked up and the dog followed me out of the van. I felt very dizzy and had to sit down, but my dog couldn't work out what was going on and started licking my face, like a scene straight out of a Lassie film.

I eventually ended up on my back with my head on the kerbstone, and though not sure what was happening to me, I knew that I had to get my dog back in the van. I managed to crawl back and secure him inside knowing that he would not let anyone near me if he was loose, then called up on my radio, gave my location shouted HELP and passed out. I vaguely woke up surrounded by police officers who believed at the time that I had been assaulted.

The Policeman's Wife

Some of the stories he had to tell at the end of a shift were incredible and fascinating and exciting but mostly brilliant because he was home with me, and had lived to tell the tale.

One particular set of nights had been busy as usual, with Jim coming home tired each morning after driving around Bristol, crisscrossing his own Division and other areas too. Saturday night was likely to have been more of the same, with the addition of weekend revelry.

That Sunday morning I woke up and checking the clock reminded myself what day it was and thought about how I would occupy my toddler so that Jim could get some sleep that morning. Resisting the temptation of a longer lie in, I showered and threw on a sweatshirt and leggings, listening for sounds of my toddler waking up. The sound I heard though, was a loud knock and the doorbell ringing, and pulling back the bedroom curtains I was surprised to see two dog vans at the drive. Jim must be working on and forgotten his key, I thought, until I saw my Mum. Slightly shocked I ran downstairs to see the silhouettes of people beyond the obscure glass. I took a breath and opened the door. My Mum stood with the Inspector and a dog handler, and as explanations began, my focus was drawn to a coloured plastic property bag being held by one of Jim's colleagues. It was large and almost opaque but I could see the outline of boots with the clothes contained in it. This is it then. That moment I hoped would never come. We had joked about his nine lives and the second or third 'nine' that he's used up during a working life of hazards and situations.

The Inspector began telling me that they don't know what happened, but Jim's in hospital and they had picked up my Mum to look after our son whilst they take me to see him. But he is ok.

Really! Why don't you tell me the truth, I thought, I can see that bag with all his clothes. I'm not a fool and I can't expect Mum to get the baby up, that's my job and he will be confused, and I need to do something normal... that I can control, that I expected to be doing this morning.

There was some light hearted joking, the sort of thing policemen do to temper serious situations but though I probably smiled, I really wasn't in the mood to be laughing.

I invited them in and asked Mum to make tea while I went up stairs to sort out my son. I put on my best dress and controlling the temptation to cry, put on a bit of my usual makeup to look respectable. It may be the last time I see him. Outwardly strong and calm (I think) I insisted on driving myself. (I never do that. Jim always drives and I go along with whatever the plan is.) The Inspector insisted on coming with me and I drove following the other dog van, the short distance to Frenchay Hospital. We could have gone anywhere as I was on automatic, and kept my eyes on the van in front, making some sort of conversation as though everything was normal.

We entered the hospital and they were talking about finding the ward number, but I could see we were following the Mortuary sign. There it was indicating right, and they carried on, still looking for a room. Well they hadn't moved him yet then.

I had been in a mortuary before, to see a post mortem. On that day there were the bodies lined up for the surgeon's day's work. Five men of retired age looking somehow similar, and unmarked and what one would expect. The other table held a young woman, a little older than me at that time, at 19 or early 20's. She had pale skin and dark tangled hair, and clogged mascara suggested that she had been crying before taking that fatal jump. Her slim body showed abrasions but the real damage was inside; ruptured spleen and other organs from the impact of hitting safety netting beneath the Clifton Suspension Bridge. Pressure had been insurmountable for that student.

We reached the door, and entering the intensive care ward, I saw him with wires attached to shaved sections of his very hairy chest, linked to monitors with lights flashing numbers and his eyes..... were open!

Two traffic officers picked me up and put me in the recovery position on the back seat of their patrol car and drove the two miles to Frenchay hospital. Though I have no recollection of this, one of the officers later told me that he thought I had died during the short journey.

I was taken to the Intensive Care Unit and assessed for a possible heart problem or stroke, and remained in hospital for a week whilst tests were done. Nothing untoward was found by the medical staff who concluded that I must have fainted. Fainted, really?..I have never fainted in my life but after being discharged I didn't feel right for a long time.

Relieved

After a week or so of sick leave, my first call was to a man armed with felling axe who was in a garden holding at bay several police officers equipped with riot shields and one officer had been struck. I was at Filton some six miles away and instead of setting out immediately, I paused, opened my sandwich box and, between Filton and Yate, I ate all my sandwiches...? Not my usual practice!

As I approached Yate the control room radioed that the axeman had been overpowered and cancelled me. The relief was immense. I didn't have to deal with what was potentially another life threatening situation, but that was the first time I had any doubts about dealing with any job that came my way as a policeman or as a dog handler.

The writing was on the wall.

Shift work takes it toll. Asleep when most are awake and awake when most are asleep. Trying to relax after a late turn, knowing that a quick change over will see you back in at 6am. Not interested in the mundane events of the day but concerned with how to keep your family (and the public) safe and protected. Getting those jobs done today because anything could happen tomorrow. Driving to make sure you get there safely. Considering the worst possible scenario and preparing for that instead of expecting the positive. Glass half empty. Life half full.

Sleeping became an issue. Like many of my colleagues I enjoyed a tot of whisky as an aid to relaxation at the end of the day. For some the tot became a bottle or more, and caused a sorry end. In comparison I knew my intake was moderate and therefore not a problem, but I was unable to sleep well and when I did my dreams became nightmares, reliving the most challenging situations and also affecting my loved ones. Sometimes I found it difficult to stay awake during the day.

As a dog handler the day shift 8am to 4pm was usually a training day for the department with at least one dog handler on day patrol covering the city. All handlers were in radio contact and could be called upon in an emergency, so the content of the day could change at any time.

My patrol van was located at Almondsbury Police Traffic department on the M5 M4 junction and on one training day I drove the eight miles to the Bower Ashton Police dog training centre. Travelling on a long elevated section of the M5, I reached the apex of the Avon bridge and momentarily fell asleep at the wheel, almost colliding with the safety barrier on the near side hard shoulder. To be so tired at 8.15a.m. was a real cause for concern and a soul-searching twenty minute drive led me to report to a supervisor on arrival, and explain what was happening to me.

I was reluctant to sign off sick as I knew that my role as a police dog handler could be jeopardised but, if I didn't, the Superintendent would order me to. After returning the dog van I drove home with my police dog, in trepidation at the thought of losing him along with my job. Discussions with the occupational health team and a review of my medical history, highlighted a succession of inconsequential illnesses that indicated a more serious problem of anxiety depressive illness, later referred to as PTSD.

After four worrying months I was retired from the police service and although I received a medical pension, a lot of adjustments were needed as I had a wife and our three year old son depending on me.

Getting Away

So that was it! Career over. Cause of stress removed. Happy days?

We lived in a modern house on the new developing town of Bradley Stoke. (Known as 'Sadly Broke' to those hit by recession) Whilst there, we had said goodbye to German Shepherd Rocky and Explosives Spaniel Sally and handed Pace back to the force for rehandling. I also said goodbye to a role that I had put my heart and soul into.

The home needed little maintenance and our toddler filled each day. A house was burgled nearby. What if I'd been on duty? There were few areas or streets that I'd not patrolled, and passing road signs linked to incidents brought those details to mind. Chased one there, nicked two there, and even recalled the full name and CRO number of some 'clients'.

I noticed potential shoplifters in every store and looked twice at everyone and everything. The sight of a patrol car or sound of sirens hammered my chest. You can take the man out of the job but not not the job out of the man.

It is possible to make changes though, and on a trip to Devon we found the perfect 'countryside house for renovation' and made the move. With peace and quiet and plenty to do, it seemed perfect for me to be 'out standing in my field', but was not without challenges. On one occasion, the window fitter, electricians and plumbers were required to vacate the building to allow for a woodworm treatment, and some pipes which should have been removed were obstructing the hall. Time was of the essence so I helped to clear the space. From my perspective I was being perfectly reasonable and not overreacting, until the plumber complained "It wasn't so much the fact that you threw all my copper pipe onto the lawn, but the distance you threw it!"

I loved my time as a dog handler working with Jason, Sally, Pace and especially Rocky, a true gentleman of a dog if there is such a thing. It was a very sad day when I had to let him go but I'm sure he is in the "Big Kennel" in the sky with his original handler Bob, making sunbeams to shine on us all.

As we said in the police force 10-10 off duty.

Acknowledgements

I would like to acknowledge the support and help received from former colleagues, friends and family who have journeyed with me, and none more so than my wife, Rose Watts, who has enabled the writing of this book and to my son, Sam Watts, for creating front cover and preparing the manuscript for publication.

I would like to acknowledge the work being carried out by the Injury On Duty Pensioners Association in educating and supporting it's members.

www.iodpa.org - Registered charity number 1174473

We are a Charitable Incorporated Organisation (association model) with members who are former police officers all medically retired with an injury on duty award (IOD). This site provides the reader with a wealth of experience, knowledge and information collated by those living with an injury pension. Those involved in IODPA cover the breadth of the UK with links to every region.

Samaritans - www.samaritans.org

Samaritans is a charity registered in England and Wales (219432) and in Scotland (SC040604) and incorporated in England and Wales as a company limited by guarantee (757372). Samaritans Ireland is a charity registered in the Republic of Ireland (20033668) and incorporated in the Republic of Ireland as a company limited by guarantee (450409).

Colleague Acknowledgments

Police Doghandler Ray Holmes and Police Dog Digger

Police Doghandler Bob Williams and Police Dog Rocky

Police Sergeant Doghandler Vern Essex, who can be seen in the training video with Jim Watts and Police Dog Jason.

Alfred Tennyson Ullysses

TO STRIVE, TO SEEK, TO FIND AND NOT TO YIELD.

Some animals were injured in the making of this memoir.

The writing-up of these events commenced at least ten years ago but was abandoned when the PC crashed.

Abbreviations

PTSD - Post-traumatic stress disorder (PTSD) is an anxiety disorder caused by very stressful, frightening or distressing events.

M.O. - Modus operandi, a method of operating

CRO - Criminal Records Office number

TIC - Taken into consideration

Printed in Great Britain
by Amazon